Puritanism

IN EARLY AMERICA

EDITED WITH AN INTRODUCTION BY
George M. Waller

Problems in American Civilization

READINGS SELECTED BY THE
DEPARTMENT OF AMERICAN STUDIES
AMHERST COLLEGE

D. C. HEATH AND COMPANY; Boston

INTRODUCTION

TODAY the term Puritan is often applied to various manifestations of American life. Sometimes the allusion is merely metaphoric, suggesting similarities between some aspect of current behavior and the ways of the New England colonists. But those who see "Puritan" traits in the lineaments of later America often go further to maintain that an actual connection exists between later American development and its Puritan heritage. In a recent study of the genesis of the American mind, Max Savelle finds Puritanism ". . . firmly rooted in the American experience and in the emerging American mind of the eighteenth century, and from New England as a center it has radiated its influence in American civilization, for good or ill, from that day to this; and the end is not yet."[1] Ralph Barton Perry concludes that "The puritans imprinted on English and American institutions a quality of manly courage, self-reliance, and sobriety. We are still drawing upon the reserves of spiritual vigor which they accumulated."[2] In fact, the postulate that Puritanism has been one of the principal influences in the development of American civilization is an assumption rarely questioned by writers of our history.

But there are many who differ over which aspects of Puritanism have been the influential ones, and many more who disagree violently over the question of whether the influence has been for good or ill. At any rate, these disputes, too great for consideration except by indirection in the limited scope of this book, have kept alive an endless curiosity about the original settlers, about the nature of Puritanism at its heyday in America in the seventeenth and early eighteenth centuries.

What is the truth about the Puritan commonwealth, Massachusetts-Bay's experiment in making religion the controlling force in civil life? Was it a perverse attempt to regulate life? One that stifled all tendency to free use of the intellect? One that willfully rejected ideas of civil liberty and the possibilities of free development? One that warped the lives of its people? Or was it a healthy product of its time, a preserver of free institutions in a new land? A cooperative effort of intelligent, vigorous leaders of thought to safeguard the heritage of European values and extend civilization despite the rigors of New World conditions?

The selections in this book represent the pros and cons. Varying with the times, the interests, and the preconceptions of individuals, opinions about the Puritans, their ideals, their aims, and their actual accomplishments have usually been highly favorable or unfavorable. Writers have seldom been lukewarm, although some have been at pains

[1] Max Savelle, *Seeds of Liberty* (New York, 1948), p. 27.

[2] Ralph Barton Perry, *Puritanism and Democracy* (New York, 1944), p. 268.

to balance their judgment. They have shown no uniformity, some coming to the problem as political historians, some as philosophers, some as literary critics, some as students of cultural and intellectual development, looking often at quite different aspects of the times they write about. The reader must weigh their views, making allowances, judging what virtue may offset what vice, to reach a conclusion generally favorable or unfavorable to the Puritans, to find his own answer to the question of whether the Puritanism of the Massachusetts-Bay colonists exercised a constructive or restrictive influence in New England colonial development.

More than a century and a quarter of American history preceded the Puritan settlement. The voyages of discovery in the late fifteenth century and during the sixteenth century gradually laid bare the eastern outlines of the American continents and were followed by scattered settlements: by the Spanish in the Central and South American lands, by the Dutch and Swedes along the Hudson and Delaware Rivers, by the French in the St. Lawrence River Valley, and by English colonists along the seaboard from Maine to Virginia. Jamestown was permanently settled in 1607. The colony of Plymouth was established in 1620 by a small band of religious radicals known as Separatists, who represented an extreme wing of the prevailing group dissatisfied with religious and civil conditions in England. Other outposts of fishermen and fur traders were to be found along the shores of the present New England.

One of these, at Cape Ann, struggled along from 1623 to 1626, when, under its leader, Roger Conant, it moved to Salem in search of better land. To this little settlement in 1628 came John Endecott

with some two score colonists and their possessions, responding to Conant's suggestion that it "might prove a receptacle for such as upon the account of religion would be willing to begin a foreign plantation" there.[3] Endecott's colonists represented the advance guard of those who were contemplating the establishment in New England of a prosperous settlement which would serve as a home and center of religious activity for those in England known as Puritans who were disillusioned with conditions in their native land. Since these Puritans were unwilling to separate from the English Church as the Pilgrims had, they were not minded to join the colony at Plymouth. Instead, a group of Puritan leaders formed themselves into the Massachusetts Bay Colony, with a royal charter granted by Charles I, and with their friends, servants, and others interested in colonization for diverse reasons, removed with their goods and chattels to the region Endecott was preparing for them. The company and charter went with them, as an effective means of preventing these instruments from falling into the control of others who might be unfriendly to the religious aims of the colony and consequently interfere with the successful establishment of the ideal Bible Commonwealth they envisioned.

It is this movement, then, with which we are mainly concerned, the history of Massachusetts Bay from its settlement in the summer of 1630 to the end of the century: the "Great Migration" of hundreds of English Puritans and their followers, led by John Winthrop and Thomas Dudley; the establishment of a virtual oligarchy of the Puritan leaders,

---

[3] Quoted in Charles M. Andrews, *The Colonial Period of American History* (New Haven, 1934), I, 353.

civil and ecclesiastical; and the banishment of those who dissented from the project of a Bible Commonwealth, culminating in the expulsion of Anne Hutchinson in 1638. A strict policy against innovation was established by a synod of the clergy in 1648 and enforced by an act of the General Court in 1651. It was only at the end of the century that the forces of opposition to the Puritan oligarchy began to assert more and more control over the colony. By that time the colony's characteristics may no longer be attributed wholly to the Puritan experiment. Of course, the culture of the "New England Way," once established, proved difficult to uproot; those men and ideas representative of Puritanism which persisted beyond the loss of the colony's charter and the substitution of a new one in 1691 may also be fairly included in our analysis of Puritan influence.

To judge the consequences of Puritanism for Massachusetts the student will want to know the answers to a host of subsidiary questions: Who were the Puritans? What were the most important characteristics of New England Puritanism? How did that of Massachusetts Bay differ from that of England? What differences existed between New Englanders and other colonial Americans? Was Puritanism more influential for the course of colonial New England than other forces like the common English heritage, or the frontier, or the recurring dissent of independent spirits like Roger Williams, Anne Hutchinson, the Quakers, and numerous others? Was the final ostensible "failure" of the Puritan Commonwealth really a failure?

Sharp divergence of opinion over these questions and over the general question of the contribution of Puritanism to New England's colonial development has always existed, as it has over the broader problem of the influence of Puritanism on later American life. The Puritans' evaluations of their own achievements, penned by William Bradford, John Winthrop, William Wood, Edward Johnson, William Hubbard, Nathaniel Ward, John Cotton, and the Mathers, met with the vigorous contemporary dissent of the unsympathetic Thomas Morton, Roger Williams, George Bishop, John Clarke, Samuel Gorton, Thomas Lechford, and others.

Nevertheless, it was the custom of loyal descendants of the Bay Colony, writing during the nineteenth century, to accept the Puritans' self-appraisal. Countless orators on commemorative occasions, joined by historians like John G. Palfrey, Henry M. Dexter, George E. Ellis, and J. A. Vinton, without blinking the facts of New England history, indeed, cataloging them at tedious length in ponderous tomes, upheld their ancestors as torchbearers of religious liberty, civil rights, political freedom, and democracy.

But even the nineteenth century did not find all New Englanders capitulating to filio-pietistic acceptance of such views. Charles Francis Adams and his brother, Brooks Adams, descendants of two American presidents, and both eminent New Englanders in their own right, challenged what they considered the "Puritan Myth," that religious liberty and political equality grew out of the Puritan spirit. Both considered that Massachusetts was held in bondage by the tyranny of the Puritan clergy and saw in the religious intolerance of Puritanism a force which made for superstition, narrow conformity, strict and meaningless formalism in religion, intellectual atrophy, a morbid and unhealthy outlook, and an arid literature, all leading straight to the excesses of the witchcraft mania and the mid-eighteenth century religious frenzies of the Great Awakening.

Present day historians have re-examined Puritanism but are still widely split in their evaluations. In general, the Puritans' detractors conclude that Puritanism was an impossible ideal and an inhuman moral and religious code. By reason of its intolerance its political, social, and religious life became rigid and formalized, bringing about intellectual stagnation and barrenness in all forms of creative endeavor. The restrictive New England way of life contained within it the seeds of its own destruction in its resistance to change and its hostility to dissent. The contribution which New Englanders were to make to American development was delayed until the Puritan oligarchy could be overcome, as it finally was. These writers agree with Charles M. Andrews, a foremost authority on colonial history:

. . . to have preserved . . . the religious doctrines of the Puritans, as shaped in the seventeenth century, to have perpetuated their ideals of government . . . and to have continued a polity based on what these men conceived was God's will in his relations to men would have served no good ends either for Massachusetts or the world at large.[4]

On the other hand, many historians seeking a sympathetic understanding of Puritanism have concluded that it was a realistic and constructive approach to life, religiously and morally, and that as such it made significant contributions to the intellectual life in the colonies and to the creative arts. Its rigorousness was a necessity in the face of external opposi-

tion, internal dissent, and the conditions of the frontier which faced the colonists. As Samuel Eliot Morison puts it, ". . . in a new country the natural alternative to intellectual puritanism is intellectual vacuity . . . or that overwhelming materialism that we find in the typical newly settled region. . . ."[5] Herbert L. Osgood, author of a monumental seven volume history of the American colonies, points out that "though we consider Puritan New England to have been narrow and intolerant, we should remember that the intellectual activity which made even that possible did not exist in the other colonies. . . ."[6] The challenge which the Puritan met was to provide an environment conducive to the effective transmission of the civilization of the Old World to the New, no easy task. Admittedly the ideal of a City of God on Earth failed, as earthly Utopias do, but was it not a good try? Did it not offer constructive answers to the perplexing questions which beset colonial times? Even though aspects of the New England Way were eventually modified, the residuum represented, its proponents aver, a lasting Puritan contribution to its own and later times.

These conflicting arguments and some of the evidence to support them are presented by leading students of our colonial past in the readings which follow. Charles A. Beard, leading off with a short article reflecting his customary stimulating iconoclasm, challenges the reader to re-examine the record. Accordingly, it is followed by a careful statement of what Puritanism was by Professor Perry Miller of Harvard University, a close and sym-

[4] Charles M. Andrews, *Our Earliest Colonial Settlements* (New York, 1933), p. 84.

[5] Samuel Eliot Morison, *The Puritan Pronaos* (New York, 1936), pp. 14–15.

[6] Herbert L. Osgood, *The American Colonies in the Seventeenth Century* (New York, 1904), I, 255.

pathetic student of the ideology of colonial New England; while a brief account
of the "Wilderness Zion" furnishes a
background of events in the colony during the seventeenth century as seen
through the eyes of T. J. Wertenbaker, a
hostile critic. Another selection from this
author is used to conclude the readings.
It represents the considered judgment of
a recent synthesizer of the history of the
Puritan oligarchy, a final word for the
Puritans' opponents. Wertenbaker denies
the good influence of the Bible State in
molding the character of New England,
and finds in its failure evidence of its
shortcomings.

Following the first two general accounts, two selections further embody
the case against the Puritans. Its consequences are detailed by Vernon Louis
Parrington, who is concerned with the
results of Puritan doctrines and practices
as expressed in the minds and personalities of the colonists, culminating in the
narrowness of the Mathers. An older
view but one which must still be reckoned with is the downright condemnation leveled by Charles Francis Adams
against both early New Englanders and
later generations of their apologists. Yet
these critics perceived that the Puritan
leaders in waging their vigorous struggle
for self-government and a church free
from English control unwittingly indoc-
trinated New Englanders with the seed
of democratic ideas far different from
professed beliefs. They hold that this
paradoxical nourishment of an illiberal
theology on the one hand with, on the
other hand, a church polity and attitudes
toward English control which were implicitly, although unconsciously, democratic, enabled New England eventually
to overcome the tyranny of Puritan rule
and emerge as a pre-eminent defender
of the ideals of the American Revolution.

Selections from two books by Samuel
Eliot Morison join issue with the foregoing antagonists in judgments on the
contribution of the Puritans to New England life, carrying further the discussion
of their influence on politics, literature,
science, and the arts.

The Mathers, father and son, and the
Salem witchcraft mania are recurrent
themes in almost every appraisal of New
England Puritanism. Analysis of these
two phenomena furnish us with something specific in our consideration of the
civilization of the Bay Colony. A selection from Marion L. Starkey's new book
provides a lively critique of both to add
to the judgments already expressed by
Parrington, Charles F. Adams, and Samuel E. Morison.

In rebuttal to those who have decried
the Puritan contribution to literature, the
next selection, from Kenneth B. Murdock's recent authoritative work, sets
forth the influences which conditioned
the writings of the Massachusetts Bay
colonists and the literary principles
which they followed.

A general, balanced estimate of the
nature and validity of the Puritans' approach to life is essayed in the selections
from Ralph Barton Perry's *Puritanism
and Democracy*. Here a philosopher
comes to the conclusion that their values
embraced truths as well as manifesting
certain blindnesses. The reader may
draw his own conclusions as to which
were more significant.

Invariably problems of the sort included in these readings raise issues
which are crucial today as they were in
colonial Massachusetts. We are faced at
present with the problem of whether increased powers for government and cen-
tralized control of economic life can gain
us enhanced security, efficiency, and
greater social benefits, or whether a re-

sultant loss of freedom intellectually, politically, and economically, along with inflexibility of institutions would deprive America of the ingredients of its greatness. What answer may be drawn from the analogy with the Puritan oligarchy? Was the strict control and discipline of the Puritan colony justified in the need to provide conditions in which the colonists could establish themselves securely in the New World, with their political institutions, their economic order, and the broad cultural patterns they were at-

tempting to transplant from the Old World? Or was there a stifling of free, creative forces which delayed the very processes of growth and development which were necessary to healthy existence? Was the colony subjected to a kind of dry rot which later generations had to struggle to overcome? Let the reader decide.

[NOTE: The statement by C. S. Lewis on p. xii is quoted from *The Screwtape Letters* (New York, 1948), p. 55, and is used with permission of The Macmillan Company.]

CONTENTS

THE CLASH OF ISSUES

Screwtape, an important official in his Satanic Majesty's "Lowerarchy," in C. S. Lewis's little classic, said of Puritanism:

> ". . . the value we have given to that word is one of the really solid triumphs of the last hundred years. By it we rescue annually thousands of humans from temperance, chastity, and sobriety of life." •
>
> — *The Screwtape Letters*

A recent historian of Puritan Massachusetts concludes:

> "No truthful historian will withhold from New England the credit due her for her part in the creation and moulding of the nation. . . . But most of the contributions were made after the fall of the Puritan oligarchy, and the men to whom the chief credit is due were not its supporters, but, on the contrary, those who rebelled against it."
>
> — T. J. WERTENBAKER: *The Puritan Oligarchy*

An historian sympathetic to the Puritans disagrees:

> ". . . the story of the intellectual life of New England in the seventeenth century is not merely that of a people bravely and successfully endeavoring to keep up the standards of civilization in the New World; it is one of the principal approaches to the social and intellectual history of the United States."
>
> — SAMUEL E. MORISON: *The Puritan Pronaos*

A philosopher attempts a balanced judgment:

> "The puritan's harsh insistence on the pre-eminent importance of salvation was suited to the exigencies of reform, or of revolution, or of migration and settlement. . . . It was not so good a gospel to live by over long periods of normal relaxation. Like all policies adapted to times of emergency, it curtailed liberty and impoverished the content of life."
>
> — RALPH BARTON PERRY: *Puritanism and Democracy*

No doubt for many of us, as Longfellow said:

> ". . . The stern old puritanical character rises above the common level of life; it has a breezy air about its summits, but they are bleak and forbidding."

Charles A. Beard: ON PURITANS

THE solemn hour approaches. It will soon be just three hundred years since the Pilgrims let go their anchor off the coast of Cape Cod. A flood of oratory will surely descend upon us. The New England societies, the Pilgrim societies, the Forebears societies, the Colonial Dames, and the French and Indian War societies, and all those who need an excuse for a night out will attend banquets given under the benign auspices of astute hotel managers. College presidents, serene, secure, solemn, and starched will rise and tell again to restless youths the story of Miles Standish and Cotton Mather. Evangelical clergymen will set aside special days for sermons and thanksgivings. The Archbishop of Canterbury (shades of Laud!) will send a cablegram to the Back Bay Brotherhood! We shall be shown again, as Henry Jones Ford (Scotch-Irish) once remarked, "how civilization entered the United States by way of New England." We shall hear again how it was the Puritans who created on these shores representative and democratic republics, wrested the sword of power from George III, won the Revolutionary war, and freed the slaves. It has ever been thus. Egomania must be satisfied and after dinner speakers must have their fees.

The flood of half truth, honest ignorance, and splendid conceit will produce an equal reaction — a cry of rage and pain from the improvers of America. Mr. H. L. Mencken will burst upon our affrighted gaze in full war paint, knife in teeth, a tomahawk dripping with ink in one hand, a stein of Pilsner in the other, and the scalps of Professors Phelps, Sherman, and Matthews hanging to his belt. He will spout a huge geyser of pishposh and set innumerable smaller geysers in motion near Greenwich Village.

In view of the clouds on the horizon and the impending deluge, it would be well to take our latitude now and find our course lest we should be blown ashore and wrecked upon the rocks of Plain Asininity. Nothing would be more sensible than to renew our acquaintance with Green, Gardiner, Prothero, Hallam, Lingard, Clarendon, Ludlow, Bradford, Usher, Bancroft, and the other serried volumes that flank the wall. The record seems to stand fairly clear: an autocratic Stuart monarchy and an intolerant ear-clipping Church, the protests of the purifiers, qui . . . receptam Ecclesiae Anglicanae disciplinam, liturgiam, episcoporum vocationem in quaestionem palam vocarunt, immo damnarunt, the propositions of Cartwright, the godliness of the independents, the Mayflower Compact, Cotton Mather's Magnalia, and all the rest.

But neither the orators nor the contemners are content with the plain record. They must show how the Puritans had all the virtues or all the vices. Once the term Puritanism had fairly definite connotations. Now it has lost them all. By the critics it is used as a term of opprobrium applicable to anything that interferes with the new freedom, free verse, psychoanalysis, or even the double entendre.

Evidently in the midst of much confusion, some definition is necessary, and for that purpose I have run through a dozen

Reprinted by permission from the *New Republic*, XXV, No. 13 (December, 1920), 15–17.

eulogiums on the Puritans (not omitting
G. W. Curtis's orations) and an equal
number of attacks on the Puritans (not
omitting Mencken's Prefaces). From
these authentic documents I have culled
the following descriptive terms applied to
Puritans. I append a table for the benefit
of the reader. Puritanism means:

Godliness	Philistinism
Thrift	Harsh restraint
Liberty	Beauty-hating
Democracy	Sour-faced fanaticism
Culture	Supreme hypocrisy
Industry	Canting
Frugality	Demonology
Temperance	Enmity to true art
Resistance to tyranny	Intellectual tyranny
Pluck	Brutal intolerance
Principle	Grape juice
A free church	Grisly sermons
A free state	Religious persecution
Equal rights	Sullenness
A holy Sabbath	Ill-temper
Liberty under law	Stinginess
Individual freedom	Bigotry
Self-government	Conceit
The gracious spirit of	Bombast
Christianity	

I look upon this catalogue and am puz-
zled to find "the whole truth." When I
think of Puritan "temperance" I am reminded of cherry bounce and also the
good old Jamaica rum which New England used to make in such quantities that
it would float her mercantile marine.
When I think of "demonology," I remember that son of Boston, Benjamin Franklin,
whose liberality of spirit even Mencken
celebrates, when he falsely attributes it
to French influence, having never in his
omniscience read the Autobiography.
When I think of "liberty and individual
freedom," I shudder to recall stories of
the New England slavers and the terrible
middle passage which only Ruskin's su-
perb imagination could picture. When I

think of "pluck and industry," I recollect
the dogged labors of French peasants,
Catholic in faith and Celtic in race. When
I see the staring words "brutal intolerance" I recall the sweet spirit of Roger
Williams, aye, the sweeter spirit of John
Milton whose Areopagitica was written
before the school of the new freedom was
established. When I read "hypocrisy" and
"canting" I cannot refrain from associating with them the antics of the late Wil-
helm II who, I believe, was not born in
Boston. So I take leave of the subject.
Let the honest reader, standing under the
stars, pick out those characteristics that
distinctly and consistently mark the Puritans through their long history.

If we leave generalities for particulars
we are equally baffled. Some things of
course are clear. The art of reading and
writing was doubtless more widely spread
in New England than in the other colonies, but that has little or no relation to
education or wisdom. Until about 1890
New England did most of the Northern
writing for "serious thinkers." It is not
necessary to name authors or magazines.
New England early had a considerable
leisure class free for excursions into the
realm of the spirit, but whether that was
the product of Puritanism or catches of
cod is an open question. Most of our histories have been written in New England,
but the monopoly has long passed. New
England contributed heavily to western
settlement, to the Union army, and to the
annual output of textiles. Puritanism did
not build our railways, construct our blast
furnaces or tunnel our hills.

But when one goes beyond so many
pages of poetry, so many volumes of history and sermons, and the Puritan Sabbath one is in a quaking bog. Critics attribute the raucous and provincial note
in our literature to the Puritans. No student of the history of civilization would

make that mistake. What have the millions of French who have lived and died in Canada produced to compare with the magnificent literature of France? How many Greek colonies scattered along the shores of the Mediterranean could rival the metropolis in sculpture or tragedy? The rusticity of the province was not monopolized by Puritans.

Take then the matter of government. The Mayflower Compact, the Fundamental Orders of Connecticut, and the Fundamental Articles of New Haven set forth a form of religious brotherhood as old as the Church at Jerusalem described in the Acts. The Pilgrims were not Puritans anyway, but even if they were they did not invent the term or the idea of a compact. The so-called democracy of the Massachusetts Bay Corporation was nothing but the democracy of an English company of merchant adventurers brought to America. What was not religious was English. Nothing was new. Nothing in the realm of ideas was contributed by the Puritans.

Consider also the spirit of our government. If we speak of American democracy, must we not think of Jefferson rather than John Adams or Fisher Ames? And Jefferson was born in Virginia, the original home of slavery, indentured servitude, an aristocracy, and an Established Church. Moreover his doctrines, especially his political views, were not as Mencken implies "importations" from France. Any schoolboy who ever heard of John Locke knows better. Was John Locke a Puritan?

Did Jefferson create American democracy? I resort to a Puritan of the Puritans, who according to authentic documents knew and loved good whiskey, Daniel Webster. He delivered an oration at Plymouth on the two hundredth anniversary of the landing of the Pilgrims, and he told more solid truth than will be found in all

the oratorical eruptions that will break forth in this harassed land next December. And what did he say? "Our New England ancestors . . . came to a new country. There were as yet no land yielding rent, and no tenants rendering service. . . . They were themselves either from their original condition or from the necessity of their common interest, nearly on a general level in respect to property. Their situation demanded a parcelling out and division of the lands and it may be fairly said that this necessary act fixed the future frame and form of their government. The character of their political institutions was determined by the fundamental laws respecting property."

For more than two hundred years the freeholder and his wife who labored with their own hands shaped the course of American development. This fact has more to do with American democracy, American art, American literature, as Mencken himself knows and says, than all the Puritanism ever imported into New England. The yeoman and his wife were too busy with honest work to give long hours to problem plays, sex stories, or the other diversions of "the emancipated age." Imagine Bernard Shaw, Gilbert Chesterton, or Baudelaire doing a turn at log rolling or at spring plowing in the stormy fields of New Hampshire! Sufficient unto the day is what comes out of it. Whoever will not try to see things as they really are need not set himself up as a critic or teacher. And let it be remembered that the Irish, Germans, Poles, Hungarians, and Jews are not the only people who can be objective, high, diaphanous, Olympian and understand "poor, crude America, with its dull, puritanical, Philistine history."

It was not the Puritans that inflicted professors and doctors of philosophy upon us and doctors' dissertations, seminars, research, and "thoroughness." It was not a Puritan nor even an Englishman who first spent five years on the gerundive in Caesar. It was not a Puritan who devised the lecture system, or professorships in English literature. The Puritan may not measure up to Mencken's ideal of art, but he did build houses that are pleasing to the eye and comfortable to live in, and he never put his kitchen midden before his front door. Let us remember also that it was not the Puritans who expelled Shelley from Oxford, and that Lincoln, of New England origin, loved a ripping story, wrote a good hand, had irregular notions about Providence, was not a Sabbatarian, and did not advocate the eighteenth amendment.

Perry Miller: THE PURITAN WAY OF LIFE

1. *The Puritan in His Age*

PURITANISM may perhaps best be described as that point of view, that philosophy of life, that code of values, which was carried to New England by the first settlers in the early seventeenth century. Beginning thus, it has become one of the continuous factors in American life and American thought. Any inventory of the elements that have gone into the making of the "American mind" would have to commence with Puritanism. It is, indeed, only one among many: if we should attempt to enumerate these traditions, we should certainly have to mention such philosophies, such "isms," as the rational liberalism of Jeffersonian democracy, the Hamiltonian conception of conservatism and government, the Southern theory of racial aristocracy, the Transcendentalism of nineteenth-century New England, and what is generally spoken of as frontier individualism. Among these factors Puritanism has been perhaps the most conspicuous, the most sustained, and the most fecund. Its role in American thought has been almost the dominant one, for the descendants of Puritans have carried at least some habits of the Puritan mind into a variety of pursuits, have spread across the country, and in many fields of activity have played a leading part. The force of Puritanism, furthermore, has been accentuated because it was the first of these traditions to be fully articulated, and because it has inspired certain traits which have persisted long after the vanishing of the original creed. Without some understanding of Puritanism, it may safely be said, there is no understanding of America.

Yet important as Puritanism has undoubtedly been in shaping the nation, it is more easily described than defined. It figures frequently in controversy of the last decade, very seldom twice with exactly the same connotation. Particularly of recent years has it become a hazardous feat to run down its meaning. In the mood of revolt against the ideals of previous generations which has swept over our period, Puritanism has become a shining target for many sorts of marksmen. Con-

From *The Puritans* by Perry Miller and Thomas H. Johnson. American Book Company, 1938. Reprinted by permission.

fusion becomes worse confounded if we attempt to correlate modern usages with anything that can be proved pertinent to the original Puritans themselves. To seek no further, it was the habit of proponents for the repeal of the Eighteenth Amendment during the 1920's to dub Prohibitionists "Puritans," and cartoonists made the nation familiar with an image of the Puritan: a gaunt, lank-haired killjoy, wearing a black steeple hat and compounding for sins he was inclined to by damning those to which he had no mind. Yet any acquaintance with the Puritans of the seventeenth century will reveal at once, not only that they did not wear such hats, but also that they attired themselves in all the hues of the rainbow, and furthermore that in their daily life they imbibed what seem to us prodigious quantities of alcoholic beverages, with never the slightest inkling that they were doing anything sinful. True, they opposed drinking to excess, and ministers preached lengthy sermons condemning intoxication, but at such pious ceremonies as the ordination of new ministers the bill for rum, wine, and beer consumed by the congregation was often staggering. Increase Mather himself — who in popular imagination is apt to figure along with his son Cotton as the arch-embodiment of the Puritan — said in one of his sermons:

Drink is in itself a good creature of God, and to be received with thankfulness, but the abuse of drink is from Satan; the wine is from God, but the Drunkard is from the Devil.[1]

Or again, the Puritan has acquired the reputation of having been blind to all aesthetic enjoyment and starved of beauty; yet the architecture of the Puritan age grows in the esteem of critics and the household objects of Puritan manufacture, pewter and furniture, achieve prohibitive prices by their appeal to discriminating collectors. Examples of such discrepancies between the modern usage of the word and the historical fact could be multiplied indefinitely.[2] It is not the purpose of this volume to engage in controversy, nor does it intend particularly to defend the Puritan against the bewildering variety of critics who on every side today find him an object of scorn or pity. In his life he neither asked nor gave mercy to his foes; he demanded only that conflicts be joined on real and explicit issues. By examining his own words it may become possible to establish, for better or for worse, the meaning of Puritanism as the Puritan himself believed and practiced it.

Just as soon as we endeavor to free ourselves from prevailing conceptions or misconceptions, and to ascertain the historical facts about seventeenth-century New Englanders, we become aware that we face still another difficulty: not only must we extricate ourselves from interpretations that have been read into Puritanism by the twentieth century, but still more from those that have been attached to it by the eighteenth and nineteenth. The Puritan philosophy, brought to New England highly elaborated and codified, remained a fairly rigid orthodoxy during the seventeenth century. In the next age, however, it proved to be anything but static; by the middle of the eighteenth century there had proceeded from it two distinct schools of thought, almost unalterably opposed to each other. Certain elements were carried into the creeds and practices of the evangelical religious revivals, but others were perpetuated by

1 *Wo to Drunkards* (Cambridge, 1673), p. 4.

2 Cf. Kenneth B. Murdock, "The Puritan Tradition in American Literature," *The Reinterpretation of American Literature* (New York, 1928), chap. V.

the rationalists and the forerunners of Unitarianism. Consequently our conception of Puritanism is all too apt to be colored by subsequent happenings; we read ideas into the seventeenth century which belong to the eighteenth, and the real nature of Puritanism can hardly be discovered at all, because Puritanism itself became two distinct and contending things to two sorts of men. The most prevalent error arising from this fact has been the identification of Puritanism with evangelicalism in many accounts, though in histories written by Unitarian scholars the original doctrine has been almost as much distorted in the opposite direction.

Among the evangelicals the original doctrines were transformed or twisted into the new versions of Protestantism that spawned in the Great Awakening of the 1740's, in the succeeding revivals along the frontier and through the back country, in the centrifugal speculations of enraptured prophets and rabid sects in the nineteenth century. All these movements retained something of the theology or revived something of the intensity of spirit, but at the same time they threw aside so much of authentic Puritanism that there can be no doubt the founding fathers would vigorously have repudiated such progeny. They would have had no use, for instance, for the camp meeting and the revivalist orgy; "hitting the sawdust trail" would have been an action exceedingly distasteful to the most ardent among them. What we know as "fundamentalism" would have been completely antipathetic to them, for they never for one moment dreamed that the truth of scripture was to be maintained in spite of or against the evidences of reason, science, and learning. The sects that have arisen out of Puritanism have most strikingly betrayed their rebellion against the

true spirit of their source by their attack upon the ideal of a learned ministry; Puritans considered religion a very complex, subtle, and highly intellectualized affair, and they trained their experts in theology with all the care we would lavish upon preparing men to be engineers or chemists. For the same reasons, Puritans would object strenuously to almost all recent attempts to "humanize" religion, to smooth over hard doctrines, to introduce sweetness and light at the cost of hardheaded realism and invincible logic. From their point of view, to bring Christ down to earth in such a fashion as is implied in statements we sometimes encounter — that He was the "first humanitarian" or that He would certainly endorse this or that political party — would seem to them frightful blasphemy. Puritanism was not only a religious creed, it was a philosophy and a metaphysic; it was an organization of man's whole life, emotional and intellectual, to a degree which has not been sustained by any denomination stemming from it. Yet because such creeds have sprung from Puritanism, the Puritans are frequently praised or blamed for qualities which never belonged to them or for ideas which originated only among their successors and which they themselves would have disowned.

On the other hand, if the line of development from Puritanism tends in one direction to frontier revivalism and evangelicalism, another line leads as directly to a more philosophical, critical, and even skeptical point of view. Unitarianism is as much the child of Puritanism as Methodism. And if the one accretion has colored or distorted our conception of the original doctrine, the other has done so no less. Descendants of the Puritans who revolted against what they considered the tyranny and cruelty of Puritan theology, who substituted taste and reason for dogma and authority and found the emotional fervor of the evangelicals so much sound and fury, have been prone to idealize their ancestors into their own image. A few decades ago it had become very much the mode to praise the Puritans for virtues which they did not possess and which they would not have considered virtues at all. In the pages of liberal historians, and above all in the speeches of Fourth of July orators, the Puritans have been hymned as the pioneers of religious liberty, though nothing was ever farther from their designs; they have been hailed as the forerunners of democracy, though if they were, it was quite beside their intention; they have been invoked in justification for an economic philosophy of free competition and laissez-faire, though they themselves believed in government regulation of business, the fixing of just prices, and the curtailing of individual profits in the interests of the welfare of the whole.[3]

The moral of these reflections may very well be that it is dangerous to read history backwards, to interpret something that was by what it ultimately became, particularly when it became several things. . . .

The Puritans were not a bashful race, they could speak out and did; in their own words they have painted their own portraits, their majestic strength and their dignity, their humanity and solidity, more accurately than any admirer has been able to do; and also they have betrayed the motes and beams in their own eyes

[3] In 1639, John Cotton condemned as a "false principle" the assertion "that a man might sell as dear as he can, and buy as cheap as he can," and Mr. Robert Keayne was fined £200 by the General Court and admonished by the church of Boston for making a profit of sixpence or more in the shilling (*Winthrop's Journal*, ed. J. K. Hosmer [New York, 1908], I, 315–318).

more clearly than any enemy has been able to point them out.

2. *The Spirit of the Age*

Puritanism began as an agitation within the Church of England in the latter half of the sixteenth century. It was a movement for reform of that institution, and at the time no more constituted a distinct sect or denomination than the advocates of an amendment to the Constitution of the United States constitute a separate nation. In the 1530's the Church of England broke with the Pope of Rome. By the beginning of Elizabeth's reign it had proceeded a certain distance in this revolt, had become Protestant, had disestablished the monasteries and corrected many abuses. Puritanism was the belief that the reform should be continued, that more abuses remained to be corrected, that practices still survived from the days of Popery which should be renounced, that the Church of England should be restored to the "purity" of the first-century Church as established by Christ Himself. In the 1560's, when the advocates of purification first acquired the name of Puritans, no one, not even the most radical, knew exactly how far the process was to go or just what the ultimate goal would be; down to the days of Cromwell there was never any agreement on this point, and in the end this failure of unanimity proved the undoing of English Puritanism. Many Puritans desired only that certain ceremonies be abolished or changed. Others wanted ministers to preach more sermons, make up their own prayers on the inspiration of the moment rather than read set forms out of a book. Others went further and proposed a revision of the whole form of ecclesiastical government. But whatever the shade or complexion of their Puritanism, Puritans were those who wanted to continue a movement which was already under way. Their opponents, whom we shall speak of as the Anglicans — though only for the sake of convenience, because there was at that time not the remotest thought on either side of an ultimate separation into distinct churches, and Puritans insisted they were as stoutly loyal to the established institution as any men in England — the Anglicans were those who felt that with the enthronement of Elizabeth and with the "Elizabethan Settlement" of the Church, things had gone far enough. They wanted to call a halt, just where they were, and stabilize at that point.

Thus the issue between the two views, though large enough, still involved only a limited number of questions. On everything except matters upon which the Puritans wanted further reformation, there was essential agreement. The Puritans who settled New England were among the more radical — though by no means the most radical that the movement produced — and even before their migration in 1630 had gone to the lengths of formulating a concrete platform of church organization which they wished to see instituted in England in place of the episcopal system. Joining battle on this front gave a sufficiently extended line and provided a vast number of salients to fight over; the gulf between the belief of these Puritans and the majority in the Church of England grew so wide that at last there was no bridging it at all. But notwithstanding the depth of this divergence, the fact still remains that only certain specific questions were raised. If we take a comprehensive survey of the whole body of Puritan thought and belief as it existed in 1630 or 1640, if we make an exhaustive enumeration of ideas held by New England Puritans, we shall find that the vast majority of them were precisely those of their opponents. In other words, Puritan-

ism was a movement toward certain ends within the culture and state of England in the late sixteenth and early seventeenth centuries; it centered about a number of concrete problems and advocated a particular program. Outside of that, it was part and parcel of the times, and its culture was simply the culture of England at that moment. It is necessary to belabor the point, because most accounts of Puritanism, emphasizing the controversial tenets, attribute everything that Puritans said or did to the fact that they were Puritans; their attitudes toward all sorts of things are pounced upon and exhibited as peculiarities of their sect, when as a matter of fact they were normal attitudes for the time. Of course, the Puritans acquired their special quality and their essential individuality from their stand on the points actually at issue, and our final conception of Puritanism must give these concerns all due importance. Yet if first of all we wish to take Puritan culture as a whole, we shall find, let us say, that about ninety per cent of the intellectual life, scientific knowledge, morality, manners and customs, notions and prejudices, was that of all Englishmen. The other ten per cent, the relatively small number of ideas upon which there was dispute, made all the difference between the Puritan and his fellow-Englishmen, made for him so much difference that he pulled up stakes in England, which he loved, and migrated to a wilderness rather than submit them to apparent defeat. Nevertheless, when we come to trace developments and influences on subsequent American history and thought, we shall find that the starting point of many ideas and practices is as apt to be found among the ninety per cent as among the ten. The task of defining Puritanism and giving an account of its culture resolves itself, therefore, into isolating first of all the larger features which were not particularly or necessarily Puritan at all, the elements in the life and society which were products of the time and place, of the background of English life and society rather than of the individual belief or peculiar creed of Puritanism.

Many of the major interests and preoccupations of the New England Puritans belong to this list. They were just as patriotic as Englishmen who remained at home. They hated Spain like poison, and France only a little less. In their eyes, as in those of Anglicans, the most important issue in the Western world was the struggle between Catholicism and Protestantism. They were not unique or extreme in thinking that religion was the primary and all-engrossing business of man, or that all human thought and action should tend to the glory of God. John Donne, Dean of St. Paul's, preached in London, "all knowledge that begins not, and ends not with his glory, is but a giddy, but a vertiginous circle, but an elaborate and exquisite ignorance";[4] the content, though not the style, of the passage might just as well come from any Puritan preacher. Both the Anglican and the Puritan were at one in conceiving of man as sinful, they both beheld him chained and enslaved by evil until liberated by the redeeming grace of Christ/ They both believed that the visible universe was under God's direct and continuous guidance, and that though effects seemed to be produced by natural causes — what at that time were called "secondary causes" — the actual government of the minutest event, the rise of the sun, the fall of a stone, the beat of the heart, was under the direct and immediate supervision of God. This conception, a fundamental one in the Puritan view of the world, was no more limited

to them than their habits of eating and drinking. John Donne said:

> The very calamities are from him; the deliverance from those calamities much more. All comes from God's hand; and from his hand, by way of hand-writing, by way of letter, and instruction to us. And therefore to ascribe things wholly to nature, to fortune, to power, to second causes, this is to mistake the hand, not to know God's hand; but to acknowledge it to be God's hand, and not to read it, to say that it is God's doing, and not to consider, what God intends in it, is as much a slighting of God, as the other.[5]

A New England parson later in the century would preach in exactly the same vein:

> His hand has made and framed the whole Fabrick of Heaven & Earth. He hath hung out the Globe of this World; hung the Earth upon nothing; drawn over the Canopy of the Heavens; laid the foundation of the earth in its place; Created that Fountain and Center of Light, Heat, & Influence in this lower World, the *Sun*. . . . The whole Administration of Providence in the Upholding and Government of all created Beings, in a way of highest Wisdom and exact Order, it is *all* His work. . . . Those notable changes in the World in the promoting or suppressing, exalting or bringing down of Kingdoms, Nations, Provinces or Persons, they are all wrought by Him. . . . The Yearly seasons, also Seed-time and Harvest, Summer and Winter, binding up and covering the earth with Frost, Ice and Snow, and the releasing and renewing of the face of the Earth again, it's His work.[6]

The great Anglican preacher said, "Even in natural things all the reason of all that is done is the power and the will of him who infused that virtue into that crea-

---

[4] Donne, *Works*, ed. Henry Alford (London, 1839), I, 278.

[5] *Ibid.*, p. 120.

[6] William Adams, *God's Eye on the Contrite* (Boston, 1685), pp. 6–7.

ture,"[7] and the president of Harvard College preached a sermon on God's governing through the natural causes that might well have taken Donne's utterance for its text.

In its major aspects the religious creed of Puritanism was neither peculiar to the Puritans nor different from that of the Anglicans. Both were essentially Protestant; both asserted that men were saved by their faith, not by their deeds. The two sides could agree on the general statement that Christians are bound to believe nothing but what the Gospel teaches, that all traditions of men "contrary to the Word of God" are to be renounced and abhorred. They both believed that the marks of a true church were profession of the creed, use of Christ's sacraments, preaching of the word — Anglican sermons being as long and often as dull as the Puritan — and the union of men in profession and practice under regularly constituted pastors. The Puritans always said that they could subscribe the doctrinal articles of the Church of England; even at the height of the controversy, even after they had left England rather than put up with what they considered its abominations, they always took care to insist that the Church of England was a "true" church, not Anti-Christ as was the Church of Rome, that it contained many saints, and that men might find salvation within it. Throughout the seventeenth century they read Anglican authors, quoted them in their sermons, and even reprinted some of them in Boston.

The vast substratum of agreement which actually underlay the disagreement between Puritans and Anglicans is explained by the fact that they were both the heirs of the Middle Ages. They still believed that all knowledge was one, that

[7] Donne, *Works*, I, 33.

life was unified, that science, economics, political theory, aesthetic standards, rhetoric and art, all were organized in a hierarchical scale of values that tended upward to the end-all and be-all of creation, the glory of God. They both insisted that all human activity be regulated by that purpose. Consequently, even while fighting bitterly against each other, the Puritans and Anglicans stood shoulder to shoulder against what they called "enthusiasm." The leaders of the Puritan movement were trained at the universities, they were men of learning and scholars; no less than the Anglicans did they demand that religion be interpreted by study and logical exposition; they were both resolute against all pretences to immediate revelation, against all ignorant men who claimed to receive personal instructions from God. They agreed on the essential Christian contention that though God may govern the world, He is not the world itself, and that though He instills His grace into men, He does not deify them or unite them to Himself in one personality. He converses with men only through His revealed word, the Bible. His will is to be studied in the operation of His providence as exhibited in the workings of the natural world, but He delivers no new commands or special revelations to the inward consciousness of men. The larger unanimity of the Puritans and the Anglicans reveals itself whenever either of them was called upon to confront enthusiasm. The selections given in this volume include Governor John Winthrop's account of the so-called Antinomian affair, the crisis produced in the little colony by the teachings of Mistress Anne Hutchinson in 1636 and 1637. Beneath the theological jargon in which the opinions of this lady appear we can see the substance of her contention, which was that she was in direct communication with the Godhead, and that she therefore was prepared to follow the promptings of the voice within against all the precepts of the Bible, the churches, reason, or the government of Massachusetts Bay. Winthrop relates how the magistrates and the ministers defended the community against this perversion of the doctrine of regeneration, but the tenor of his condemnation would have been duplicated practically word for word had Anne Hutchinson broached her theories in an Anglican community. The Anglicans fell in completely with the Puritans when both of them were confronted in the 1650's by the Quakers. All New England leaders saw in the Quaker doctrine of an inner light, accessible to all men and giving a perfect communication from God to their inmost spirits, just another form of Anne Hutchinson's blasphemy. John Norton declared that the "light of nature" itself taught us that "madmen acting according to their frantick passions are to be restrained with chaines, when they can not be restrained otherwise."[8] About the same time George Hickes, Dean of Worcester, was advocating that Quakers be treated likewise in England, and he ended a sermon upon them by calling them "Imposters, or enthusiasts, and Blasphemers of the Holy Ghoast."[9] Enthusiasts, whether Antinomian or Quaker, were proposing doctrines that threatened the unity of life by subduing the reason and the intellect to the passions and the emotions. Whatever their differences, Puritans and Anglicans were struggling to maintain a complete harmony of reason and faith, science and religion, earthly dominion and the government of God. When we immerse our-

[8] *The Heart of N-England Rent at the Blasphemies of the Present Generation* (Cambridge, 1659), p. 39.

[9] Paul Elmer More and Frank Leslie Cross, *Anglicanism* (1935), pp. 68, 84.

selves in the actual struggle, the difference between the Puritan and the Anglican may seem to us immense; but when we take the vantage point of subsequent history, and survey religious thought as a whole over the last three centuries, the two come very close together on essentials. Against all forms of chaotic emotionalism, against all over-simplifications of theology, learning, philosophy, and science, against all materialism, positivism or mechanism, both were endeavoring to uphold a symmetrical union of heart and head without impairment of either. By the beginning or middle of the next century their successors, both in England and America, found themselves no longer capable of sustaining this unity, and it has yet to be re-achieved today, if achieved again it ever can be. The greatness of the Puritans is not so much that they conquered a wilderness, or that they carried a religion into it, but that they carried a religion which, narrow and starved though it may have been in some respects, deficient in sensuous richness or brilliant color, was nevertheless indissolubly bound up with an ideal of culture and learning. In contrast to all other pioneers, they made no concessions to the forest, but in the midst of frontier conditions, in the very throes of clearing the land and erecting shelters, they maintained schools and a college, a standard of scholarship and of competent writing, a class of men devoted entirely to the life of the mind and of the soul.

Because the conflict between the Puritans and the Churchmen was as much an intellectual and scholarly issue as it was emotional, it was in great part a debate among pundits. This is not to say that passions were not involved; certainly men took sides because of prejudice, interest, irrational conviction, or for any of the motives that may incite the human race to conflict. The disagreement finally was carried from the field of learned controversy to the field of battle. There can be no doubt that many of the people in England, or even in New England, became rabid partisans and yet never acquired the erudition necessary to understand the intricate and subtle arguments of their leaders. A great number, perhaps even a majority, in both camps were probably not intelligent or learned enough to see clearly the reasons for the cause they supported. Thomas Hooker, the clerical leader of the settlement of Connecticut — and therefore the dominant figure in that community — said frankly, "I can speak it by experience, that the meaner ordinary sort of people, it is incredible and unconceivable, what Ignorance is among them."[10] This being the case, we who are today being made all too familiar with the horrors of the art of "popularization," can only marvel at how little allowance the divines made for the ignorance or the simplicity of the average man in the addresses and sermons they delivered to him. It is true, several Anglicans began to feel, after the dispute became acrimonious, that the wind of doctrine ought perhaps to be tempered to the uneducated lamb; the authorities ordered parish priests not to discuss the more difficult points of speculation before all the

people.[11] The Puritans would not show their people any such mercy. They endeavored to assist the feebler understandings of their congregations by using the simplest and most comprehensible style, by employing a schematic organization for their sermons, with heads and subheads so clearly marked that earnest listeners could take notes and study the points during the week, and by eschewing Latin quotations or glittering phrases that might distract attention from content to form. But these were the only sort of crutches that Puritan ministers would allow to the rank and file for helping them over the hard parts of divinity. Of course many texts from scripture permitted sermons that were relatively simple and ethical, but others raised perplexing enigmas, discussion of which the Medieval Church had restricted to the schools; Puritans took each kind as it came and did not flinch from struggling in the pulpit with the difficult ones any more than from expounding the more obvious. Thomas Hooker told his people that they

[10] *The Soules Preparation for Christ* (London, 1632), p. 70; the sermons in this volume were delivered in England, so that Hooker was here speaking of the level of knowledge among the English people, which was of course much lower than among the select group that settled New England; New England Puritans were undoubtedly much more skilled in following the logic of theology, and they received a thorough and lifelong course of instruction in Sunday sermons and Thursday lectures. Even so, as Winthrop points out in describing the Antinomian agitation, the debate on the theology soon got over the heads of the many.

[11] The Anglican disposition to refrain from discussing the unfathomable mysteries of the creed before the laity was reinforced by a strategic consideration; the people enjoyed listening to highly technical discussions of subtle points and flocked to Puritan sermons for that reason. The English officials believed that Puritan sermons simply inflamed popular passions without elevating the public intelligence, and therefore endeavored to restrict the discussion of unanswerable questions. As the controversy widened the leading Anglicans turned against the theology of rigorous predestination and reprobation — which had been generally accepted by the first bishops of Elizabeth's reign — and identified Puritan theology with the Puritan program in church and state; the effect on the Puritans was to make them all the more determined that no subject, no matter how involved, should be kept out of the pulpits, and that the people should be lifted by main force to the highest possible pitch of understanding. Particularly were they resolved that predestination should be thoroughly thrashed out for the benefit of the populace.

were responsible for acquiring a certain amount of knowledge if they expected to be saved:

Its with an ignorant sinner in the midst of all means as with a sick man remaining in an Apothecaries shop, ful of choycest Medicines in the darkest night: though there be the choycest of all receipts at hand, and he may take what he needs, yet because he cannot see what he takes, and how to use them, he may kill himself or encrease his distempers, but never cure any disease.[12]

The wonder is that by and large the populace did yield their judgments to those who were supposed to know, respected learning and supported it, sat patiently during two- and three-hour sermons while ministers expounded the knottiest and most recondite of metaphysical texts. The testimony of visitors, travelers, and memoirs agrees that during the Puritan age in New England the common man, the farmer and merchant, was amazingly versed in systematic divinity. A gathering of yeomen and "hired help" around the kitchen fire of an evening produced long and unbelievably technical discussions of predestination, infant damnation, and the distinctions between faith and works. In the first half of the seventeenth century the people had not yet questioned the conception of religion as a difficult art in which the authority of the skilled dialectician should prevail over the inclinations of the merely devout. This ideal of subjection to qualified leadership was social as well as intellectual. Very few Englishmen had yet broached the notion that a lackey was as good as a lord, or that any Tom, Dick, or Harry, simply because he was a good,

honest man, could understand the Sermon on the Mount as well as a Master of Arts from Oxford, Cambridge, or Harvard. Professor Morison has shown that the life of the college in New England was saved by the sacrifice of the yeomen farmers, who contributed their pecks of wheat, wrung from a stony soil, taken from their none too opulent stores, to support teaching fellows and to assist poor scholars at Harvard College, in order that they and their children might still sit under a literate ministry "when our present Ministers shall lie in the Dust."[13]

When we say that the majority of the people in the early seventeenth century still acceded to the dictation of the learned in religion and the superior in society, we must also remark that the Puritan leaders were in grave danger of arousing a revolt against themselves by their very own doctrines. Puritans were attacking the sacerdotal and institutional bias which had survived in the Church of England; they were maintaining a theology that brought every man to a direct experience of the spirit and removed intermediaries between himself and the deity. Yet the authority of the infallible church and the power of the bishops had for centuries served to keep the people docile. Consequently when the Puritan leaders endeavored to remove the bishops and to deny that the Church should stand between God and man, they ran the hazard of starting something among the people that might get out of hand. Just as the Puritan doctrine that men were saved by the infusion of God's grace could lead to the Antinomianism of Mrs. Hutchinson, and often did warrant the simple in concluding that if they had God's grace

[12] *The Application of Redemption* (London, 1659), pp. 89–90; these sermons were delivered in Connecticut.

[13] Morison, *The Founding of Harvard College* (1935), p. 318; *Harvard College in the Seventeenth Century*, p. 28.

in them they needed to pay no heed to what a minister told them, so the Puritan contention that regenerate men were illuminated with divine truth might lead to the belief that true religion did not need the assistance of learning, books, arguments, logical demonstrations, or classical languages. There was always a possibility that Puritanism would raise up a fanatical anti-intellectualism, and against such a threat the Puritan ministers constantly braced themselves. It was no accident that the followers of Mrs. Hutchinson, who believed that men could receive all the necessary instructions from within, also attacked learning and education, and came near to wrecking not only the colony but the college as well.[14] Edward Johnson, stout militia captain of the town of Woburn, and no intellectual, set forth the anguish of soul through which he passed while the citizens of Boston were under the spell of "Jezebel"; he was particularly shocked to hear one of the heretics say flatly, "I had rather hear such a one that speakes from the meere motion of the spirit, without any study at all, then any of your learned Scollers, although they may be fuller of Scripture."[15] Puritanism was forever giving rise to such rebellions against its own ideal of learned religion; the experience of Massachusetts with the Hutchinsonians in the 1630's was only a premonition of what England was to encounter in the 1650's, when the Civil Wars generated not one form of Antinomianism but a thousand....

Both Cromwell and the New England leaders were face to face with a problem as old as the history of the Christian Church. Throughout the Middle Ages there had been such stirrings among the

14 Morison, *The Founding of Harvard College,* chap. XIII.

15 *The Wonder-working Providence,* ed. J. F. Jameson (New York, 1910), p. 128.

people as those to which Mrs. Hutchinson or the Fifth Monarchy Men gave voice. The great scholastic synthesis always remained incomprehensible to the vulgar, who demanded to be fed again and again with the sort of religious sustenance they craved. The Reformation drew upon these suppressed desires. Common men turned Protestant primarily because Protestantism offered them a religion which more effectively satisfied their spiritual hunger. Yet in Europe theologians and metaphysicians retained the leadership and kept Protestantism from becoming merely an emotional outburst. They supplied it with a theology which, though not so sophisticated as scholastic dogma, was still equipped with a logic and organon of rational demonstration. Though Protestantism can be viewed as a "liberation" of the common man, it was far from being a complete emancipation of the individual. It freed him from many intellectual restraints that had been imposed by the Church, but it did not give him full liberty to think anything he pleased; socially it freed him from many exactions, but it did not permit him to abandon his traditional subjection to his social and ecclesiastical superiors. The original settlers of New England carried this Protestantism intact from Europe to America. Except for the small band that was driven into exile with Anne Hutchinson, and one or two other groups of visionaries who also were hustled across the borders into Rhode Island, the rank and file did follow their leaders, meekly and reverently. Captain Johnson probably represents the average layman's loyalty to the clergy. The New England "theocracy" was simply a Protestant version of the European social ideal, and except for its Protestantism was thoroughly medieval in character.

It was only as the seventeenth century came to a close that the imported structure began to show the strain. In Europe social tradition had conspired with the ministers to check enthusiasts in religion and "levellers" in society; in England the authorities, whether Anglican or Puritan, royal or Cromwellian, were able to suppress the assault upon the scholarly and aristocratic ideal. In America the character of the people underwent a change; they moved further into the frontier, they became more absorbed in business and profits than in religion and salvation, their memories of English social stratification grew dim. A preacher before the General Court in 1705 bewailed the effects of the frontier in terms that have been echoed by "Easterners" for two hundred years and more; men were no longer living together, he said, in compact communities, under the tutelage of educated clergymen and under the discipline of an ordered society, but were taking themselves into remote corners "for worldly conveniences." "By that means [they] have seemed to bid defiance, not only to Religion, but to Civility it self: and such places thereby have become Nurseries of Ignorance, Prophaneness and Atheism."[16] In America the frontier conspired with the popular disposition to lessen the prestige of the cultured classes and to enhance the social power of those who wanted their religion in a more simple, downright and "democratic" form, who cared nothing for the refinements and subtleties of historic theology. Not until the decade of the Great Awakening did the popular tendency receive distinct articulation through leaders who openly renounced the older conception, but for half a cen-

tury or more before 1740 its obstinate persistence can be traced in the condemnations of the ministers.

The Puritan leaders could withstand this rising tide of democracy only by such support as the government would give them — which became increasingly less after the new charter of 1692 took away from the saints all power to select their own governors and divorced the state and church — or else by the sheer force of their personalities. As early as the 1660's and 70's we can see them beginning to shift their attentions from mere exposition of the creed to greater and greater insistence upon committing power only to men of wisdom and knowledge. William Hubbard in an election sermon of 1676 told the citizens that piety alone in a ruler was not enough; magistrates should be such "as by the benefit of natural parts Experience, Education, and study, have advantage above others to be acquainted with the affairs of the world abroad, as well as with the Laws and Customes of their own people at home."[17] By the beginning of the eighteenth century the task of buttressing the classified society, maintaining the rule of the well-trained and the culturally superior both in church and society seems to have become the predominant concern of the clergy. Sermon after sermon reveals that in their eyes the cause of learning and the cause of a hierarchical, differentiated social order were one and the same. For example, Ebenezer Pemberton, who was a tutor at Harvard College and then colleague minister with Samuel Willard at the Old South Church, delivered a funeral sermon upon the death of the Honourable John Walley, member of the council and judge, in 1711. Judge Walley, said Pemberton, rendered his country

---

16 Joseph Easterbrooks, *Abraham the Passenger* (Boston, 1705), p. 3; cf. Increase Mather as early as 1677: "People are ready to run wild into the woods again and to be as Heathenish as ever, if you do not prevent it" (*A Discourse Concerning the Danger of Apostacy* [Boston, 1679], 2d ed., 1685, p. 104).

17 *The Happiness of a People* (Boston, 1676), p. 28.

great service; there are various ways in which the country can be served. One of them is by the promotion of "good literature":

This is necessary for the true prosperity and happiness of a people. *Greece* and *Rome* are more renowned for the flourishing state of learning in them, than for their arms. This has for ever been in highest esteem among civilized nations. . . . The more of good literature civil rulers are furnished with, the more capable they are to discharge their trust to the honour and safety of their people. And learning is no less necessary, as an ordinary medium to secure the glory of Christ's visible kingdom. Without a good measure of this the truth can't be explained, asserted and demonstrated; nor errors detected and the heretick baffled . . . When ignorance and barbarity invade a generation, their glory is laid in the dust; and the ruin of all that is great and good among them will soon follow.[18]

A second way in which the welfare of the nation is served is by each and every person's keeping to his proper station:

This intends that we keep within the *line* and *place,* that providence has set us . . . We must not without God's call quit our post, thrust our selves into *anothers province,* with a conceit that *there* we may best serve, and promote the good of the world. But herein observe the will of God by keeping to the service that belongs to our station, which providence has made our peculiar business. Thus every man is to serve his generation by moving in his own orb; and discharging those offices that belong to that order that the government of heaven has assigned him to.[19]

Leadership by the learned and dutiful subordination of the unlearned — as long as the original religious creed retained its

18 *Sermons and Discourses on Several Occasions* (London, 1727), pp. 212–213.

19 *Ibid.*

hold upon the people these exhortations were heeded; in the eighteenth century, as it ceased to arouse their loyalties, they went seeking after gods that were utterly strange to Puritanism. They demanded fervent rather than learned ministers and asserted the equality of all men.

Thus Puritanism appears, from the social and economic point of view, to have been a philosophy of social stratification, placing the command in the hands of the properly qualified and demanding implicit obedience from the uneducated; from the religious point of view it was the dogged assertion of the unity of intellect and spirit in the face of a rising tide of democratic sentiment suspicious of the intellect and intoxicated with the spirit. It was autocratic, hierarchical, and authoritarian. It held that in the intellectual realm holy writ was to be expounded by right reason, that in the social realm the expounders of holy writ were to be the mentors of farmers and merchants. Yet in so far as Puritanism involved such ideals it was simply adapting to its own purposes the ideals of the age. Catholics in Spain and in Spanish America pursued the same objectives, and the Puritans were no more rigorous in their application of an autocratic standard than King Charles himself endeavored to be — and would have been had he not been balked in the attempt.

✿   ✿   ✿

5. *Estimations*

The Puritan attitude toward the Bible, to the extent that it was a preservation of intellectual values within the dogmatism, may elicit our hearty approbation. But when we come to the content of the dogma, to what the Puritan insisted the Bible did teach, and to what he expected the regenerate man to find reasonable, in short, when we come to Puritan theology, many persons encounter an insuperable stumbling block to an unqualified approval of Puritan thinking. Not only does the conventional picture of the Puritan creed seem exceedingly unattractive to twentieth-century taste, but the idea of theology in any form is almost equally objectionable. In most secondary accounts Puritans are called Calvinists, and then and there discussion of their intellectual life ceases. Dr. Holmes's "One-Hoss Shay" is deemed a sufficient description.

It is true, the Puritans were Calvinists, if we mean that they more or less agreed with the great theologian of Geneva. They held, that is, that men had fallen into a state of sin, that in order to be saved they must receive from God a special infusion of grace, that God gives the grace to some and not to others out of His own sovereign pleasure, and that therefore from the beginning of time certain souls were "predestined" to heaven and the others sentenced to damnation. But if the New Englanders were Calvinists, it was because they happened to agree with Calvin; they approved his doctrine not because he taught it, but because it seemed inescapably indicated when they studied scripture or observed the actions of men. The sinfulness of the average man was a fact that could be empirically verified, and in itself demonstrated that he needed divine grace in order to be lifted above himself; the men who did receive what they thought was an influx of grace learned by experience that only in such an ecstasy of illumination did truth become thoroughly evident and completely understandable. Obviously the experience was given to relatively few men; therefore God, who is outside time and who is omniscient, must have known from the beginning of time who would and who would not achieve it. This is the law

of life; some men are born rich and some poor, some intelligent and some stupid, some are lucky and others unfortunate, some are happy and some melancholy, some are saved and some are not. There is no reason but that God so ordained it.

The Lord to shew the soveraign freedom of his pleasure, that he may do with his own what he wil, and yet do wrong to none, he denyes pardon and acceptance to those who seek it with some importunity and earnestness . . . and yet bestowes mercy and makes known himself unto some *who never sought him*.[20]

Puritan theology, therefore, is simply a statement in dogmatic guise of a philosophy of life, wherein it is held on the one hand that men must act by reason and abide by justice, and strive for an inward communication with the force that controls the world, but on the other hand that they must not expect that force always to be cribbed and confined by their conceptions of what is reasonable and just. There is an eternal obligation upon men to be equitable, fair, and good, but who can say that any such morality is also binding on the universe? There are certain amenities which men must observe in their dealings with men, but who can say that they must also be respected by the tiger, by the raging storm, by the lightning, or by the cancer? It is only when the theology of "predestination" is seen in these less technical terms that its vitality as a living faith and its strength as a sustaining philosophy become comprehensible.

But the theology of New England was not simply Calvinism, it was not a mere reduplication of the dogmas of the *Institutes*. What New Englanders believed

20 Thomas Hooker, *The Application of Redemption*, p. 299.

was an outgrowth, as we have seen, of their background, which was humanistic and English, and it was conditioned by their particular controversy with the Church of England. Simon-pure Calvinism is a much more dogmatic, anti-rational creed than that of the Congregational parsons in Massachusetts. The emigrants went to New England to prove that a state and a church erected on the principles for which they were agitating in England would be blessed by God and prosper. The source of the New England ideology is not Calvin, but England, or more accurately, the Bible as it was read in England, not in Geneva.

Though, of course, the controversy in England was a political, social, and economic one, it was also the intellectual dispute we have outlined. We might summarize it at this point by saying that in order to harmonize reason and scripture, the Anglican endeavored to reduce the doctrines imposed by scripture to the barest minimum; the Puritan extended scripture to cover the whole of existence and then set himself to prove the content of all scripture essentially reasonable. Only with this definition of origins and tendencies in mind can we read Puritan theology aright. In order to demonstrate that the content of scripture was comprehensible to reason, the Puritan theorists worked out a substantial addition to the theology of Calvinism which in New England was quite as important as the original doctrine. This addition or elaboration of the Calvinist doctrine is generally called the "Covenant Theology," or the "Federal Theology." There is no necessity here for examining it in detail.[21] It was a special way of reading scripture so that the books assembled in the Bible could all be seen

to make sense in the same way. The doctrine held that after the fall of man, God voluntarily condescended to treat with man as with an equal and to draw up a covenant or contract with His creature in which He laid down the terms and conditions of salvation, and pledged Himself to abide by them. The covenant did not alter the fact that those only are saved upon whom God sheds His grace, but it made very clear and reasonable how and why certain men are selected, and prescribed the conditions under which they might reach a fair assurance of their own standing. Above all, in the covenant God pledged Himself not to run athwart human conceptions of right and justice; God was represented while entering the compact as agreeing to abide by certain human ideas. Not in all respects, not always, but in the main. I have said that any Puritan would have subscribed to Laud's argument concerning the authority of scripture; it is now necessary to add that if called upon to discuss the question himself, the Puritan would not go about it in the same way. He would not make a distinction between testimonies brought in from another realm of experience besides faith, between rational confirmations and the act of belief, but he would begin with scripture itself, the object of faith and the measure of reason. His principle argument for the satisfaction of the reason would be that once the Bible is believed by faith, it appears wholly and beautifully rational; it contains a consistent doctrine, that of the covenant, which makes it at once the source of belief and the fountain of reason.

To find equivalents in modern terms for the ideas we have been discussing is well-nigh impossible. To translate seventeenth-century issues into twentieth-century phrases, when they cannot possibly mean the same things, is to forego any accurate

---

21 Cf. Perry Miller, "The Marrow of Puritan Divinity," *Publications of the Colonial Society of Massachusetts*, XXXII, 247–300.

understanding of them. The results of modern historical investigation and textual criticism have made fantastic, even for those who believe the scripture to be the word of God, acceptance of it in anything like the spirit of the seventeenth century. But if we cannot find a common denominator for equating the ideas of the Puritans with ideas of today, we may possibly get at them by understanding the temperament, the mood, the psychology that underlay the theories. If Puritanism as a creed has crumbled, it can be of only antiquarian significance to us, but if Puritanism is also a state of mind, it may be something closer home.

There is probably no admirer of Puritanism so blindly devoted that he will not find the Anglican apologists in some respects much more attractive. The richness of their culture, the catholicity of their taste, the calmness of their temper, the well-controlled judgment, the mellow piety, and above all the poetry of Richard Hooker and Jeremy Taylor are qualities which unhappily are not too conspicuous in the pages reprinted in this volume. There is an air about these men of breadth and wisdom, they do not labor under terrific and incessant pressure, they are not always taut under the critical scrutiny of an implacable taskmaster. Simple humanity cries at last for some relief from the interminable high seriousness of the Puritan code, the eternal strenuousness of self-analysis, and the never-ending search of conscience. Though it is a great mistake to think the Puritans could not forget their theology and enjoy themselves, and though Nathaniel Ward proves that they could possess a rollicking sense of humor, the general impression conveyed by Puritan writing is that of men who lived far too uninterruptedly upon the heights of intensity. Perhaps the most damning feature of their intensity was that it could

become, over a period of time, as conventional and as stereotyped as worldliness itself. Thomas Shepard, telling the story of his conversion, has a vivid and living sense of the eternal presence of God, but Samuel Sewall, moralizing over God's grace while feeding his chickens, is at best quaintly amusing, and when he bears down with the authority of scripture on the question of wigs he becomes tiresome, as Madam Winthrop undoubtedly felt. There was almost always an element of narrowness, harshness, and literal-mindedness associated with Puritanism, enough to justify some of the criticisms of the bishops and some of the condemnations that have been made on the Puritan spirit in more recent times.

The strength of Puritanism was its realism. If we may borrow William James's frequently misleading division of the human race into the two types of the "tough-minded" and the "tender-minded," and apply it with caution, it may serve our purposes. Though there were undoubtedly men in the Church of England, such as John Donne, whom we would have to describe as "tough," and a number of Puritans who would fit the description of "tender," yet in the main Anglicans such as Hooker and Taylor are quite clearly on the side of the more tender-minded, while the Puritan mind was one of the toughest the world has ever had to deal with. It is impossible to conceive of a disillusioned Puritan; no matter what misfortune befell him, no matter how often or how tragically his fellowmen failed him, he would have been prepared for the worst, and would have expected no better. At the same time, there was nothing of the fatalist about him; as so often happens in the history of thought, the believers in a supreme determining power were the most energetic of soldiers and crusaders. The charge of Cromwell's Ironsides was, on that particular score, proof positive of the superiority of the Puritan over the Anglican, and the Indians of New England learned to their very great sorrow how vehement could be the onset of troops who fought for a predestined victory. There was nothing lukewarm, half-hearted, or flabby about the Puritan; whatever he did, he did with zest and gusto. In that sense we might say that though his life was full of anguish of spirit, he nevertheless enjoyed it hugely. Existence for him was completely dramatic, every minute was charged with meaning. And when we come to an end of this roll call of characteristics, the one which yet remains the most difficult to evoke was his peculiar balance of zeal and enthusiasm with control and wariness. In his inner life he was overwhelmingly preoccupied with achieving a union with the divine; in his external life he was predominantly concerned with self-restraint. Compare, for example, these two passages from Thomas Hooker: the first in the vein of subjective rapture:

So, I would have you do, loose your selves, and all ordinances, and creatures, and all that you have, and do, in the Lord Christ. How is that? Let all bee swallowed up, and let nothing be seene but a Christ . . . As it is with the Moone and Starres, when the Sunne comes, they loose all their light, though they are there in the heavens still; and as it is with rivers, they all goe into the Sea, and are all swallowed up of the Sea; and yet there is nothing seene but the Sea . . . So let it bee with thy Soule, when thou wouldest finde mercy and grace.[22]

And then this admonition:

I know there is wilde love and joy enough in the world, as there is wilde Thyme and other herbes, but we would have garden love and garden joy, of Gods owne planting.[23]

No wonder the Puritan has been something of a puzzlement and a trial to the Gentiles. He was a visionary who never forgot that two plus two equals four; he was a soldier of Jehovah who never came out on the losing side of a bargain. He was a radical and a revolutionary, but not an anarchist; when he got into power he ruled with an iron hand, and also according to a fundamental law. He was a practical idealist with a strong dash of cynicism; he came to New England to found the perfect society and the kingdom of the elect — and never expected it to be perfect, but only the best that fallible men could make. His creed was the revealed word of God and his life was the rule of moderation; his beliefs were handed down from on high and his conduct was regulated by expediency. He was a doctrinaire and an opportunist. Truth for him had been written down once and for all in a definitive, immutable, complete volume, and the covers closed to any further additions; thereupon he devoted all the energies he could spare from more immediate tasks to scholarship and interpretation. He lived in the world according to the principles that must govern this world, with an ever-present sense that they were only for the time being and that his true home was elsewhere. "There is," said John Cotton, "another combination of vertues strangely mixed in every lively holy Christian, And that is, Diligence in worldly businesses, and yet deadnesse to the world; such a mystery as none can read, but they that know it." The Puritan ideal was the man who could take all opportunities, lose no occasions, "and bestir himselfe for profit,"

22 *The Soules Humiliation* (London, 1638), p. 77.

23 *The Soules Implantation* (London, 1637), p. 158.

and at the same time "bee a man dead-hearted to the world." He might wrest New England from the Indians, trade in the seven seas, and speculate in lands; "yet his heart is not set upon these things, he can tell what to doe with his estate when he hath got it."[24]

The most serious of charges laid against the Puritans has been their supposed deficiency in aesthetic perceptions. Because they did not want men to fix their veneration upon worldly things, they had no use for sculpture, distrusted the arts when they were prized merely for their sensuous appeal, were contemptuous of the beautiful ritual and ornamentation of the Church of England. The poet George Herbert, defending the habiliment of his church against what he thought the trappings of the Church of Rome, found the plainness of Puritan worship going much too far in the other direction:

> She in the valley is so shie
> Of dressing that her hair doth lie
>   About her eares;
> While she avoids her neighbour's pride,
> She wholly goes on th'other side,
>   And nothing wears.[25]

The New Model Army has incurred infamy with posterity for hacking to pieces the furnishings of cathedrals. But the asperity of the Puritan discipline and the Puritan distrust of merely sensuous beauty did not mean that the Puritan was without an aesthetic of his own, or that he was hostile to beauty. John Preston defined beauty in characteristic Puritan fashion: "Beauty that consists in a conformity of all the parts";[26] Thomas

Hooker said that sin "defaceth the beautiful frame, and that sweet correspondence and orderly usefulness the Lord first implanted in the order of things."[27] The Puritan conceived of beauty as order, the order of things as they are, not as they appear, as they are in pure and abstract conception, as they are in the mind of God. He spoke of his church polity, his bare, crude churches, without altars or choirs, foursquare and solid, as lovely; they were so to him because they incarnated the beauty of the one polity Christ had ordained. His conception of the beautiful was, like Plato's, the efficient order of things; in that sense, he held indeed that beauty is truth, and truth beauty, though he did not think that was quite all he needed to know in life.

When the historian thus attempts to consider Puritanism in all its ramifications, he finds himself at the end hesitating to deliver judgment upon it, or to be wholly satisfied that it has passed into the limbo of anthologies. Certainly we can look upon the disappearance of some features with no regrets, and only deplore some others where they still survive. We have had enough of the Puritan censoriousness, its tendency to make every man his brother's keeper. When the Puritan habit of probing into the soul has degenerated into the "New England conscience" — where it is apt to remain as a mere feeling that everything enjoyable is sinful — then the ridicule heaped upon Puritan inhibitions becomes a welcome antidote. Certainly many amenities of social life have increased in New England, and in America, in direct proportion as Puritanism has receded. But while we congratulate ourselves upon these ameliorations, we cannot resist a slight fear that much of what has taken the place of

[24] *Christ the Fountaine of Life* (London, 1651), pp. 119–120.

[25] *Works*, ed. George Herbert Palmer (New York, 1905), III, 103.

[26] *The New Creature*. (London, 1633), p. 52.

[27] *The Application of Redemption*, p. 59.

Puritanism in our philosophies is just so much failure of nerve. The successors of Puritanism, both the evangelicals and the rationalists, as we survey them today, seem to have been comparatively sentimental, to have lacked a stomach for reality. The optimism and cheerfulness to which the revolters against Puritanism turned now threaten to become rather a snare and a delusion than a liberation. "Science" tells us of a world of stark determinism, in which heredity and environmental conditioning usurp the function of the Puritan God in predestining men to ineluctable fates. It is, indeed, true that the sense of things being ordered by blind forces presents a different series of problems than does the conception of determination by a divine being; no matter how unintelligible the world might seem to the Puritan, he never lost confidence that ultimately it was directed by an intelligence. Yet even with this momentous difference in our imagination of the controlling power, the human problem today has more in common with the Puritan understanding of it than at any time for two centuries: how can man live by the lights of humanity in a universe that appears indifferent or even hostile to them? We are terribly aware once more, thanks to the revelation of psychologists and the events of recent political history, that men are not perfect or essentially good. The Puritan description of them, we have been reluctantly compelled to admit, is closer to what we have witnessed than the description given in Jeffersonian democracy or in transcendentalism. The Puritan accounted for these qualities by the theory of original sin; he took the story of the fall of man in the Garden of Eden for a scientific, historical explanation of these observable facts. The value of his literature today cannot lie for us in his explanation; if there is any, it must rest in the accuracy of his observations.

Thomas Jefferson Wertenbaker:

THE FALL OF THE WILDERNESS ZION

ALTHOUGH the English government in permitting the settlement of New England was actuated by economic considerations, a large proportion of the settlers themselves journeyed into the wilderness chiefly for religion's sake. Not only did they wish to escape persecution in England, but they were determined to establish in America a retreat for all of like faith with themselves, a bulwark against the forces of Antichrist. "All other churches of Europe have been brought under desolations," they said, "and it may be feared that the like judgements are coming upon us; and who knows but God hath provided this place to be a refuge for many, whom he means to save out of the General Destruction." They hoped to better their condition in a new and fertile country, of course, for the decline of industry and the lack of employment made conditions difficult in England. "The whole earth is the Lord's garden, . . . why then should we stand starving here for places of habitation, and in the mean time suffer whole countries . . . to lye waste without any improvement?"

But their minds were fired chiefly with the hope of establishing a Bible commonwealth, sealed against error from without and protected from schism from within. "What can be a better or nobler work, and more worthy of a Christian," they said, "than to erect and support a reformed particular Church in its infancy. . . ."[1] It is incorrect to infer that most of the colonists were not deeply religious merely because it is found that church members were in the minority. Many righteous Puritans were unable to state an overwhelming religious experience which would qualify them for membership, yet they were sympathetic with the church's purpose.

In so large a movement some were unquestionably impelled by one motive, some by another. Of the thousands of men and women who landed on the New England shores in the years from 1629 to 1640, there were many who felt little sympathy with the erection there of a powerful theocracy, some who had come on the representations of the shipping agents as to the opportunities to win a competence in America.[2] But they were forced to conform to the wishes of the leaders, men of the type of John Winthrop, John Cotton, John Norton and John Wilson. This latter group enjoyed a prestige which was born not only of superior education but of an extraordinary talent for leadership. Schooled in the bitter controversies of the day, hardened in the fires of adversity, they were well fitted to play the role of Moses in the removal of this modern host to the promised land. "Though the reformed church, thus fled into the wilderness, enjoyed not the miraculous pillar," Cotton Mather tells us, "we enjoyed many a person, in whom the good spirit of God gave a conduct unto us, and mercifully dispensed those directing, defending, refreshing influences, which were as necessary for us, as any that the celebrated pillar of cloud and fire could have afforded."

These men were intent on establishing a theocracy in which their tenets and their form of worship should be upheld by the hand of the law. They were not Separatists but Church of England men, and what they designed was an established church in New England. At the very outset they made it clear that "they did not separate from the Church of England, nor from the ordinances of God there, but only from the corruptions and disorders of that Church; that they came away from the Common-Prayer and Ceremonies."[3] On another occasion they called the Anglican church "their dear mother, desiring their friends therein to recommend them unto the mercies of God in their constant prayers, as a Church now springing out of their own bowels, nor did they think that it was their mother who turned them out of doors, but some of their angry brethren, abusing the name of their mother."[4]

The migrating preachers had fought in the old country, not only for the right to worship as they chose in their individual

---

[1] Cotton Mather, *Magnalia Christi Americana* [London, 1702] (Hartford, 1853), I, 65, 70.

[2] A good discussion of the character and motives of the colonists is found in Carl Becker, *Beginnings of the American People* (W. E. Dodd, ed., *The Riverside History of the United States*, Boston, 1915, I), chap. iii.

[3] Cotton Mather, *Magnalia*, I, 74.

[4] Cotton Mather, *Magnalia*, I, 76.

churches but also for control of the Anglican establishment. Had they succeeded, they would have forced the church into complete conformity with their views, driving out those who persisted in opposing them. Failing in their efforts, they removed to America where there could be no opposition to their plans. Having set up their reformed church, having transplanted what they believed to be the true Anglican church to their new homes, they intended to protect it from innovation by the authority of the civil law. "We came hither because we would have our posterity settled under the pure and full dispensations of the gospel; defended by rulers that should be of ourselves."[5] These words, delivered at one of the notable election sermons, give the keynote of the movement. Their church they intended to buttress by a state especially designed for its protection.

Obviously toleration had no part in such a plan. It is a singular perversion of history which attributes ideals to the prime movers in this great migration that they themselves would have been the first to repudiate. The fact that the Puritans deserted their homes to settle in the wilderness in order to worship God as they chose led even Charles II to suppose that they had openly espoused the principles of toleration. That the same mistake should be so common today, when religious freedom has been widely accepted as a principle essential to the welfare of mankind, is perhaps natural, if not inevitable. "On no subject dealt with among us," says a son of New England in an address before the Massachusetts Historical Society, "in lectures, orations, sermons, poems, historical addresses, and even in our choice school literature, has there been such an amount of crude,

sentimental, and wasteful rhetoric, or so much weak and vain pleading, as on this. . . . The root of the whole error, common alike to those who censure and those who defend those ancient Fathers, is the assumption that they came here mainly to seek, establish, and enjoy liberty of conscience."[6]

The sermons and published writings of the founders of Massachusetts make it clear that they never entertained the thought of opening the doors of their new Zion to those who differed from them. So far from being champions of toleration, they opposed it bitterly. " 'T is Satan's policy, to plead for an indefinite and boundless toleration," said Thomas Shepard.[7] Urian Oakes denounced religious freedom as the "first born of all Abomination,"[8] while Increase Mather sternly rebuked the "hideous clamours for liberty of Conscience." John Norton denounced liberty of worship as liberty "to answer the dictates of the errors of Conscience in walking contrary to Rule. It is a liberty to blaspheme, a liberty to seduce others from the true God. A liberty to tell lies in the name of the Lord." The Puritan community thought that heretics should have only the liberty to leave. As Nathaniel Ward said, "All Familists, Antinomians, Anabaptists, and other Enthusiasts shall have free liberty to keepe away from us."[9] We gain an insight into the depth of this feeling from the dismay of Edward Johnson when he found Massachusetts rent by the Anne Hutchinson heresy. He had fled to what he thought would be a

[6] The Reverend George E. Ellis.

[7] Lindsay Swift, "The Massachusetts Election Sermons," Col. Soc. of Mass., *Publs.*, I, 400.

[8] Swift, "The Massachusetts Election Sermons," 401.

[9] Nathaniel Ward, *Simple Cobbler of Aggawamm* (London, 1647), 3–12, *passim*.

[5] Cotton Mather, *Magnalia*, I, 219.

safe retreat from heresy, where his soul could rest in peace free from the dread of error. Now he found controversy raging within the very walls of the new Zion, and he had to choose once more, at the peril of his soul, between truth and falsehood.

We fail to grasp the spirit of these men unless we realize that they considered themselves a chosen people, one to whom God had revealed himself and had led to the promised land far from the sins and corruptions of the Old World. "The ministers and Christians, by whom New England was first planted, were a chosen company of men," says Cotton Mather, "picked out of, perhaps, all the counties of England, and this by no human contrivance, but by a strange work of God upon the spirits of men that were, no ways, acquainted with one another, inspiring them as one man, to secede into a wilderness, they knew not where."[10] William Stoughton expressed the same idea in his famous statement that "God hath sifted a nation, that he might send choice grain into this wilderness." God's concern for the settlement had been lovingly manifested by striking the Indians with a plague a few years before the migration, thus making the waste places safe for his children.[11] Such an attitude does not conduce to toleration. Convinced that he had been selected by God to receive and expound the truth, the Puritan minister could but look upon those who opposed him as minions of Satan. . . .

The Massachusetts leaders were intent upon establishing, not a government representative of the wishes of the people but an oligarchy in which the clergy would have the deciding voice. The civil authorities of the new state were to serve as handmaidens to the church, and the ministers, although themselves not holding public office, were to be the final depository of power in the colony. This power they exercised chiefly through their control of the franchise. No man was to vote who was not a member of the church, and no man could be a member of the church until he had been admitted by the clergy. The clergy, in turn, took care to admit none who were in opposition to the established order. "In as much as very much of an Athenian democracy was in the mould of the government by the royal charter," says Cotton Mather, "Mr. Cotton effectually recommended it unto them, that none should be electors, nor elected therein, except as were visible subjects of our Lord Jesus Christ, personally confederated in our churches. In these, and many other ways, he propounded unto them an endeavour after a theocracy, as near as might be, to that which was the glory of Israel, the peculiar people."[12]

As for democracy, the New England fathers dreaded it as a form of government inconsistent with the rule of the best and most pious men. "Democracy I do not conceive that God did ever ordain as a fit government for either church or commonwealth," says John Cotton. "If the people be governors, who shall be governed? As for monarchy and aristocracy, they are both clearly approved and directed in the Scriptures. . . . He setteth up theocracy . . . as the best form of government in the commonwealth as in the church."[13] Winthrop

---

10 Cotton Mather, *Magnalia*, I, 240.

11 Edward Johnson, *Wonder-Working Providence of Sions Saviour in New England* [London, 1654] (J. F. Jameson, ed., *Original Narratives of Early American History*, N. Y., 1906–), 41.

12 Cotton Mather, *Magnalia*, I, 266.

13 Thomas Hutchinson, *The History of the Colony of Massachusetts-Bay* (Boston, 1764–1828), I, 437.

agreed heartily, averring that democracy had no warrant in Scripture and that "among nations it has always been accounted the meanest and worst of all forms of government."

Thus the earnest men who led the Puritan exodus planned their new Bible commonwealth and thus they built it. Composed in large measure of persons of like faith, protected from invasion by its very isolation, guided by the clergy and by magistrates in close sympathy with them, this wilderness Zion was the culmination of their fondest hopes. Yet from the first the theocracy found itself faced by a multitude of difficulties, which threatened its supremacy and slowly undermined its strength.

The first of these was that love for self-government so universal among Englishmen. All the reverence, all the love, all the admiration which the people had for their leaders, did not reconcile them to the loss of their liberty. In the early days of the colony the outstanding leader was John Cotton. This remarkable man has been spoken of as "the unmitred pope of a pope-hating people." What he advised from the pulpit was usually enacted into law. The chronicler of Christ's wonders in America says that Cotton was the great director, "the father and glory of Boston."[14] Yet even the influence of John Cotton could not prevent a strong faction of the people from demanding that in their new home they should not be deprived of their rights and liberties. According to the charter all important matters of government were left to the discretion of the stockholders, or freemen, in the general court. Only twelve

of these freemen had come to Massachusetts in 1630, and all had been made magistrates. Since they were in full sympathy with the leading clergymen, and supported them in all their policies for both church and state, the arrangement constituted the government by the best which Winthrop and Cotton so earnestly advocated. Democratic it was not. When the first general court convened in October, 1630, the magistrates had shrunk in number to eight, and this small group were confronted with a demand from one hundred and nine of their fellow settlers to be admitted as freemen. These men were doubtless all Puritans, but they could see in their demand for citizenship nothing inconsistent with the dictates of their religion.

The magistrates postponed action on this petition until the spring. In the meanwhile they decreed that the assistants and not the freemen should make laws and elect the governor, and that the assistants should hold office during good behavior. This left the freemen only the right to select new assistants when vacancies occurred. The applicants agreed to this arrangement although it left them only the husks of real citizenship, and for some months more the little body of magistrates continued to tax and legislate. In 1632, however, when the assistants voted a levy for fortifications, the town of Watertown entered a vigorous protest. Under the leadership of their minister the people passed a resolution "that it was not safe to pay moneys after that sort, for fear of bringing themselves and posterity into bondage."[15] Governor Winthrop, greatly disturbed at this show of insubordination, summoned the Water-

[14] Cotton Mather, *Magnalia*, I, 252. The biographical chapter on Cotton (252–286) is very interesting. See also E. D. Mead, "John Cotton's Farewell Sermon," Mass. Hist. Soc., *Proceeds.*, ser. 3, I, 105.

[15] John Winthrop, *History of New England* (J. K. Hosmer, ed., in J. F. Jameson, ed., *Original Narratives of Early American History*, N. Y., 1906–ʃ), I, 74.

town men before him, and after they had made their submission, pardoned them. But the other towns were not less concerned at the limitations set upon their liberty. When the general court met in May, the body of the freemen voted that the governor and his assistants must be elected each year, and that every town should elect two delegates to act with them in levying taxes.

Although this was a long step toward representative government, it still left the deputies without a hand in making laws. In 1634 they assumed this right also. In May two men from each of the eight towns met in Boston and demanded to view the charter of the colony. Winthrop dared not refuse, and they at once called his attention to the fact that the charter gave the making of laws to the whole body of freemen. When the general court met a few days later, three deputies appeared from each town, ready to demand their rightful share in the government. Against this action the magistrates and leading ministers protested. The very foundations of the newly established theocracy seemed to be crumbling. John Cotton threw the full weight of his influence in favor of upholding the established order, pleading that the Bible clearly showed that the magistrates ought to hold office for life. But the freemen, so far from yielding, refused to reëlect Winthrop governor, and actually imposed fines upon some of the magistrates for abuse of power. They then decreed that henceforth the general court, consisting of the governor, the assistants and deputies elected by the towns, alone should have the right to tax, make laws and admit freemen.

Thus, four years after the Massachusetts Bay charter was brought to America, the government was changed from a narrow oligarchy to what appeared to be a little republic. Yet, even after the establishment of representative government, very little real liberalism existed, and the theocracy still ruled almost supreme. The freemen were only a small part of the population and the law forbidding the admission of nonchurch-members was rigidly enforced. Moreover, the prestige of the few leading laymen of the colony was such that they were selected as magistrates over and over again. John Cotton insisted "that a magistrate ought not to be turned into the condition of a private man, without just cause, and be publicly convict, no more than the magistrate may not turn a private man out of his freehold, etc., without like public trial." The idea became fixed that every official should be reëlected unless convicted of misconduct. Consequently the governor and his assistants continued to represent only the narrowest aristocratic clique in the colony, and the deputies a comparatively small body of voters, picked by the ministers from church members.

The theocratic form of government not only created internal dissension, but it was a leading cause in weakening Massachusetts by the withdrawal of several congregations to the Connecticut Valley. The liberal views of Thomas Hooker were so greatly at variance with those of Winthrop and Cotton that he could not rest at ease in his Newtown settlement. "There is a great disunion of judgement in matters of religion amongst good ministers and people which caused Mr. Hooker to remove," wrote the Reverend R. Stansby to John Wilson, "and that you are so strict in the admission of members to your church, that more than halfe are out of your church in all your congregations, and that Mr. Hooker before he went away preached against that."[16] Winthrop ex-

[16] Letter of April 17, 1637, Mass. Hist. Soc., *Colls.* VII, ser. 4, 10–11.

postulated with Hooker about the danger of "referring matters of counsel or judicature to the body of the people," arguing that "the best part is always the least, and of that part the wiser part is always the lesser." Hooker replied that to leave all power in the hands of rulers who were not responsible to the people, was to invite tyranny. I "must plainly profess if it was in my liberty, I should choose neither to live nor leave my posterity under such a government. . . . A general councel chosen by all, I conceive under favour most suitable to rule and most safe for the relief of the people."[17]

Although those who favored representative government had won a certain measure of success, schismatics and heretics at first could do nothing. The magistrates and ministers were adamant against attempts to break down the unity of their "City of God on earth." Yet both schism and heresy were prompt in showing themselves. In 1631 the scholarly and liberal Roger Williams arrived, and accepted a pastorate at Salem. An avowed Separatist, he at once attacked the established order for not renouncing fellowship with the Church of England. Besides inveighing against legal oaths and against the validity of titles to land granted by the general court, he also denounced the union of church and state, declaring from the pulpit that the magistrates had no right to punish Sabbath breaking or other violations of the first four commandments.

This open attack upon the theocracy could not be passed over. The ministers rendered their judgment "that he who should obstinately maintain such opinions, whereby a church might run into heresy, apostasy, or tyranny, and yet the civil magistrate could not intermeddle,"

was too dangerous to be tolerated.[18] Williams was cited to appear before the authorities, and after a trial was sentenced to banishment. The decree was suspended until spring, on condition that he refrain from attempting to spread his opinions. This he was unable to do, and when the magistrates decided to keep him on shipboard pending the next sailing for England, he escaped through the frozen forests to the Narragansett Bay region. The theocracy had won an easy victory, but one which was costly because achieved by appealing to the civil authorities. Schism for the moment had been blocked, but physical force cannot prevent the growth of divergent opinions, and before long heresy reappeared in a far more dangerous form.

Anne Hutchinson, who had been a parishioner of John Cotton in England, is described by Winthrop as a woman of "ready wit and bold spirit." Several years after her arrival in Boston she began the dangerous practice of holding meetings in her house to rehearse and discuss the sermon of the previous Sunday. From this she passed to comparing the teachings of the clergymen, and then to the evolution of a doctrine of her own. The ministers were expounding a covenant of works, she maintained, whereas the Bible showed that salvation was based on a covenant of grace. Although Winthrop wrote that "no man could tell (except some few who knew the bottom of the matter) where any difference was,"[19] he and the other leaders of the theocracy understood clearly enough that her ideas were inconsistent with the established order. The covenant of grace made religion a matter of direct communication between man and his Maker, while the

---

[17] G. L. Walker, *Thomas Hooker* (N. Y., 1891), 121–122.

[18] Winthrop, *History of New England*, I, 162.

[19] Winthrop, *History of New England*, I, 209.

covenant of works required only obedience to a prescribed code of which the minister was the official interpreter. Should the former doctrine secure wide acceptance, not only would unity be lost, but a stunning blow would be struck at the theocracy.

For a time Boston supported Mrs. Hutchinson with something like unanimity. Even the great John Cotton was inclined to embrace her doctrines. The religion of love which she preached was more in keeping with his naturally kindly nature than the established tenets of law and judgment. But he drew back in time. John Wheelwright, Mrs. Hutchinson's brother-in-law, and young Harry Vane bore the brunt of the battle. The former was summoned before the general court, and although he refused to answer questions because the proceedings were held in secret, was found guilty of sedition and contempt. To weaken the influence of Boston, a resolution was passed transferring the next court of elections to Newtown. When the vote was taken, the orthodox party succeeded in restoring Winthrop to the governorship. Boston, however, sent as its deputies Vane, Coddington and Hoffe, all favorable to Mrs. Hutchinson. The court at first refused to seat them, but when Boston held a new election and returned them again, "the Court not finding how they might reject them, they were admitted." In the following summer the clergy met in synod and condemned as erroneous and blasphemous the Hutchinson heresies. At the November court Wheelwright was disfranchised and banished, while other members of the dissenting faction were severely punished. Mrs. Hutchinson was "banished from out this jurisdiction as being a woman not fit for our society."[20]

In this way was the church purged of heresy, and the theocracy saved from what to its leaders seemed the most deadly peril. It is folly to condemn these men for bigotry and intolerance. They had given up their homes and had fled into the wilderness for the purpose of establishing a society free from error. How natural, then, that they should have combated what they considered error, when to their horror they found that it had followed them across the Atlantic. "Two so opposite parties could not contain in the same body without hazard of ruin to the whole," said Winthrop. Conformity was gained, but only at the cost of a bitter struggle which left scars that were slow to heal. Theocracy was so weakened that another great heresy might shatter it.

Though for some time no such heresy arose from within, the ministers soon found themselves confronted with a peril from without. In 1656 Quaker missionaries invaded New England with the avowed purpose of making converts. The democratic leanings of the Quakers, their refusal to accord especial respect to magistrates, their denial of the need of an established clergy, combined to make them obnoxious to the Puritan leaders. When Mary Fisher and Ann Austin arrived in Boston, the colony was stirred to its foundations. "Why was it that the coming of two women so shook ye, as if a formidable army had invaded your borders?" George Bishop inquired of the magistrates.[21] But the magistrates would undoubtedly have been less dismayed at the invasion of an armed host. Powder and shot could only imperil men's lives; the Quakers were assaulting their souls. We gain an insight into the state of mind of these stern Puritans, not so much from

[20] J. T. Adams, *The Founding of New England* (Boston, 1922), 171.

[21] George Bishop, *New England Judged by the Spirit of God* (London, 1703), 2.

their action in arresting these women, denouncing their doctrines and burning their books, as from the care they took to board up the windows of their cell so that the prisoners could not preach to the people. After five weeks of imprisonment they were shipped back to Barbados whence they had come.[22]

A few days later eight more Quakers arrived from London. Governor Endicott immediately put them in prison and at the first opportunity sent them out of the country. In October the general court fixed the fine of any master who should bring in a Quaker at £100, and declared that the Quaker himself should be severely whipped. By a later enactment the offender's tongue was to be bored with a hot iron, his ears cut off, he was to be banished, and if he returned, to be executed. New Haven, Plymouth and Connecticut also passed severe laws against the Quakers, but the death penalty was prescribed by Massachusetts alone. Rhode Island, under the leadership of Roger Williams, would have none of this persecution. A band of Quakers who landed at Newport were received with kindness. But the other colonies, fearing that the missionaries would use Rhode Island as a base of operations, entered a vigorous protest. Pointing out that the "contagion" could easily spread across the borders, they threatened to take strong action "to prevent the aforesaid mischief."[23]

The reply of Williams might well have given pause to the Massachusetts magistrates and ministers. We "finde that in those places where these people, aforesaid, in this colony, are most of all suffered to declare themselves freely, and are only opposed by arguments in discourse, there they least of all desire to come . . . surely we find that they delight to be persecuted by civil powers, and where they are soe, they are like to gain more adherents by the conseyte of their patient sufferings."[24] The Rhode Island assembly answered in similar vein, reiterating their intention to uphold freedom of conscience which they prized as their greatest happiness.

The Massachusetts magistrates continued their pitiless warfare against the invaders. In September, 1659, Mary Dyer, William Robinson and Marmaduke Stevenson, who had come to Boston courting martyrdom, were all banished. Mrs. Dyer reached Rhode Island, whence she immediately returned, but the two men went only to Salem before facing about. All were sentenced to death. Robinson and Stevenson were hanged, but Mrs. Dyer, after her hands and legs had been bound, her face covered and the rope adjusted about her neck, received word that she had been reprieved. Once more she was sent to Rhode Island, but the efforts of her family to keep her there failed. In the spring she came back to Boston where she too was executed. In November, 1660, another Quaker, William Leddra, suffered the same fate.

---

[22] It must be remembered, however, that the Quakers were rather trying, judged by any standard. One woman, to evidence humility, was wont to exhibit herself in an old sackcloth gown with her face smeared with grease and lamp black; two others, though generally of modest deportment, went naked to church and market place "as a sign." See Bishop, *New England Judged*, 377, 383, and the summary of the *Persecution in New England* in J. G. Palfrey, *History of New England* (Boston, 1892), II, 449, 483; also Charles Deane, "Report on the Belknap Donation," Mass. Hist. Soc., *Proceeds.*, III (1855–1858), 320.

[23] United Colonies of New England, *Acts*, II, 180.

[24] J. R. Bartlett, comp., *Records of the Colony of Rhode Island and Providence Plantations in New England, 1636–1792* (Providence, 1856–1865), I, 376.

Though the theocracy went to these extremes, the battle was going against them. Endicott and Norton had good reason to realize that Roger Williams had been more farseeing than they, for the sufferings of the Quakers won for them the sympathy of thousands who had only contempt for their doctrines. A few days before the execution of Leddra, Wenlock Christison, another Quaker, strode into the court room, and looking into the face of Endicott, said to him, "I came here to warn that you should shed no more innocent blood, for the blood that you have shed already cries to the Lord for vengeance to come upon you."[25] He was seized and brought to trial. The magistrates debated long as to what should be done, for public sentiment was turning rapidly against them; but for Endicott there was no hesitancy. Pounding the table he shouted out, "You that will not consent, record it. I thank God I am not afraid to give judgement." Christison was condemned to death, but the sentence was never carried out. Partly from fear of interference from the crown, partly because of the evident opposition of the people, the persecution had to take a milder form. There were no more executions.

It was a severe defeat for the theocracy. The ideal of a Puritan commonwealth walled in against heresy had broken down. The suffering Quakers had proved that the New World did not offer so safe a refuge from the "poison of error" as the leaders of the exodus had hoped. Moreover, it had been made apparent that there were limits beyond which the people of Massachusetts would not follow the magistrates and ministers. The sight of a suffering Quaker, stripped to

the waist and tied to a cart's tail, his back clotted with blood from frequent whippings, trudging through snow and ice, could but cause revulsion in men's minds against the system which was responsible for it. The Puritan leader in the days of his exile and his sacrifices was an inspiring figure; the Puritan persecutor seemed in contrast unlovely indeed.

In addition, the conflict brought interference from England, and with it the threat of an early termination of the charter upon which the established order was based. Charles II, displeased at the executions, gave orders that the vein of innocent blood opened in his dominions should be closed. The English Quakers actually chartered a ship to carry this message to New England and in six weeks delivered it into Endicott's hands. Accordingly, the laws against heresy were modified, so that many mouths were "opened which were before shutt."

Charles's quarrel with the Massachusetts government was by no means limited to the question of toleration for the Quakers. When this monarch found himself fixed on the throne of his fathers, he turned his attention to colonial matters. Although the policy of his government found its chief expression in the navigation acts, his advisers were also intensely interested in political and social conditions within the individual provinces. When they became aware that Massachusetts had made itself almost independent of the crown, that power there had fallen into the hands of a narrow theological group, that the laws of England were disregarded, the oath of allegiance neglected, the Anglican worship forbidden, they at once took steps to reëstablish the king's authority in the colony. The struggle which ensued lasted for nearly three decades and ended only with the overthrow of the Stuarts. So

25 William Sewel, *The History of the Rise, Increase, and Progress of the Christian People Called Quakers* (N. Y., 1844), I, 338.

long as Charles I was uncertain of his ground in England, he refrained from pushing matters to an issue in Massachusetts, contenting himself with warnings, threats against the charter and the sending of agents to represent him in the colony. The magistrates on their part adopted a policy of procrastination. The king's commands were not openly flouted, but there were constant evasions and delay. When the Long Parliament was dissolved, the theocracy was still supreme in political and ecclesiastical affairs in Massachusetts, and paid to the crown but a shadowy homage.

With the advent of the second Stuart despotism the situation suddenly changed. The unprincipled but astute Charles II, having freed himself from the domination of Parliament by accepting a pension from Louis XIV, devoted the last years of his life to the task of ending liberty both in England and America. . . .

Had Charles confined his attack to the narrow theocratic group in Massachusetts, he would have found powerful support within the colony itself. But he was bent not only upon overthrowing the established order but upon substituting for it the despotic rule of the crown. The people were not to benefit by this transfer of power and even the forms of representative government which had persisted under the old régime were to be swept away in the new. Edmund Andros, who was made governor-general of all New England despite the guarantees of the Connecticut and Rhode Island charters, trampled ruthlessly upon the rights held most sacred by Englishmen. In conjunction with his council he made laws, gave judicial decisions and ordered the collection of taxes. The Massachusetts general court was abolished, and every freeholder was made uneasy by the threat to revoke existing land grants.

Fortunately the tyranny of Charles II and James II in New England proved short-lived. The English nation rose in 1688, drove James into exile and granted the throne to his daughter Mary and her husband, William of Orange. The Glorious Revolution is a landmark in the history of English liberty, a landmark between the period in which the theory of divine right received widespread acceptance, and the period of parliamentary supremacy. In America, especially in New England, the effects were not less far-reaching. The old Massachusetts theocracy which was demolished to make room for royal absolutism was not fully restored when absolutism in its turn was overthrown. Increase Mather went to England to plead for the renewal of the original charter, but fortunately for Massachusetts he was not successful. Mather claimed to be the representative of the whole people; yet we know that public sentiment, while hoping for the restoration of the former status of semi-independence, by no means favored the old narrow administration in local affairs. In other words, the people wanted both autonomy and political liberty, only one of which they had enjoyed prior to the second Stuart despotism, and neither under the rule of Andros. The resolution passed by Watertown in May, 1689, asking that the number of freemen "be inlarged farther than have been the Custom of this Colony formerly," was no doubt representative of opinion throughout Massachusetts.

They had their wish. The new charter, which was issued in 1691, instituted a royal government not unlike that of Virginia. There was to be a representative assembly, while the franchise was based, not on church membership, but on property holdings. The crown appointed the governor, who had the power to veto bills of the assembly, appoint judges and other officials, and put the laws into execution. Members of the council were nominated by the legislature and confirmed by the governor. Religious freedom for Protestants was guaranteed. Thus was established a new order distinctly more liberal than that under which Massachusetts had lived during the past six decades. The power of the clergy was not completely crushed; the social and political structure of the colony was not revolutionized. A full century and more was to pass before Massachusetts became in any real sense democratic. But the old buttressed Bible commonwealth, the Zion which had been the dream of Winthrop and Cotton and for which they had made such sacrifices, was gone forever....[26]

The decline of the theocracy manifested itself even more clearly in the loss of moral prestige than in the loss of political power. The sermons of the clergy in the last two decades of the seventeenth century are filled with references to the sinfulness of the day and the inattention paid to religion. "I saw a fearful degeneracy, creeping, I cannot say, but rushing in upon these churches, . . ." said Cotton Mather, in his *Magnalia*.[27] "I saw a visible shrink in all orders of men among us, from that greatness, and that goodness, which was the first grain that our God brought from three sifted kingdoms. . . . What should be done for the stop, the turn of this degeneracy?" "Let us, the children of such fathers," wrote John Higginson, "lament our gradual degeneracy from that life and power of Godliness, that was in them, and the many pro-

voking evils that are amongst us." Samuel Torry, so early as 1674, considered the golden age of New England as gone forever. "Truely, so it is, the very heart of New-England is changed and exceedingly corrupted with the sins of the Times," he said, "there is a Spirit of Profaneness, a Spirit of Pride, a Spirit of Worldliness, a Spirit of Sensuality, a Spirit of Gain-saying and Rebellion, a Spirit of Libertinism, a Spirit of Carnality, Formality, Hypocrisie and a Spiritual Idolatry in the Worship of God."[28]

Such was New England as it seemed to the more illiberal preachers of the day. It is easy for the modern mind to translate what they termed rebellion and gainsaying into a spirit of liberalism, the alleged gross licentiousness into merely a natural reaction against the iron bonds of the Puritan moral code. But they were quite right in seeing in the general tendencies of the day a gradual weakening of the influence which formerly had made the people follow their leadership with such unquestioning faith. The Halfway Covenant, introduced in 1657, which had allowed baptism to children of pious parents who yet had had no definite religious "experience," seemed to many a terrific inroad upon orthodoxy; and they were not altogether wrong, for it marked a faint beginning of reaction. The example of Rhode Island and the Providence Plantations, the only community in Christendom where anyone might explain as he would the universe and his relation to it, must have roused some doubts as to the perfection of the surrounding New England system.[29]

---

[26] For a brief general account, see H. L. Osgood, *The American Colonies in the Seventeenth Century* (N. Y., 1904–1907), III, chaps. xiii-xiv.

[27] Cotton Mather, *Magnalia*, I, 249.

[28] In his election sermon of that year at Weymouth, Mass. Lindsay Swift, "The Massachusetts Election Sermons," Col. Soc. of Mass., *Publs.*, I, 402.

[29] Maryland in its toleration act of 1649 insisted upon professed belief in the Trinity; it was almost

It must be remembered that from the first many persons settled in New England from economic rather than religious motives. Cotton Mather relates that once a Massachusetts minister, who was preaching to a congregation in the northeast region, urged them to continue a "religious people from this consideration that otherwise they would contradict the main end of planting this wilderness; whereupon a well-known person, there in the assembly, cryed out, Sir, you are mistaken, you think you are preaching to the people at the Bay; our main end was to catch fish."[30]

Even at Boston itself there were many who had come to better their fortunes rather than to escape persecution. With the development of trade and industry this group received gradual accessions until a separate merchant class had developed. Between the merchant and the clergyman there was a distinct and growing divergence of interests. The former looked out upon the whole world, his vessels wandered from the West Indies to England, and from Chesapeake Bay to the Mediterranean; he learned to know the Catholic Spaniard, the Anglican Virginian, the Quaker of Pennsylvania, and found good in them all. He had no sympathy with the policy which would make of New England a Zion, walled against the contagions of a sinful world. When Boston made it illegal for townsmen to "entertaine any strangers into their houses for above 14 days" without special permission from the authorities, it aroused the merchants to protest.

We find the pious Edward Johnson, so early as 1650, expressing alarm at the growing spirit of commercialism. Merchants and vintners "would willingly have had the Commonwealth tolerate divers kinds of sinful opinions to intice men to come and sit down with us, that their purses might be filled with coyn, the civil Government with contention, and the Church of our Lord Christ with errors."[31] As the century grew older the merchant class increased both in numbers and influence. The prosperity which they brought to New England, the outlet they offered for its products and the employment they gave to thousands of workers, rendered them formidable opponents. The ministers railed at them and warned them that they must not attempt innovations. "New England is originally a plantation of Religion, not a plantation of Trade," thundered Higginson in his election sermon of 1663. "Let Merchants and such as are increasing Cent per Cent remember this."[32] But the merchant class added a leaven to public opinion which the clergy could not ignore and found it difficult to combat. During the Salem witchcraft delusion it was Thomas Brattle and Robert Calef, both merchants, who had the common sense to see the folly of the inquisition and the bravery to denounce the justices and the ministers for their part in it.

The closing years of the seventeenth century witnessed in Massachusetts a far-reaching change. The experiment of a Bible commonwealth had definitely failed; the influence of the clergy in civil government, although by no means entirely eliminated, was greatly restricted; their hold upon the hearts and minds of the people distinctly weakened.

---

inevitable that a Catholic proprietor under an English government should be tolerant, especially when his fellow churchmen were in a minority in the colony.

[30] Cotton Mather, *Magnalia*, I, 66.

[31] Johnson, *Wonder-Working Providence*, 254.

[32] John Higginson, *The Cause of God and His People in New England* (1663), 11, quoted in Col. Soc. of Mass., *Publs.*, I, 398.

From the first the theocracy was doomed to defeat because it set itself against men's natural instincts; and natural instincts cannot permanently be suppressed. During the half century of its supremacy the theocratic establishment had to endure a succession of shocks. The struggle for representative government, the Roger Williams and Anne Hutchinson heresies, the Quaker invasion, the annulling of the old charter, the defeat in the witchcraft prosecutions, each played an important part in the overthrow.

More powerful than any one incident was the slow, almost imperceptible change which was coming over men's minds, the trend toward rationalism, the development of liberalism, the widening of human sympathies. This movement found no corresponding development among the old school of churchmen. So far from attempting to keep in step with the times, to shape their theology in conformity with new ideals and new points of view, they remained rigid and unyielding. Regarding the leaders of the exodus as saints, they sought to perpetuate their tenets and to pattern their lives after them. In this they failed, for the ability of the early fathers to move the hearts of men lay in their creative force. John Winthrop and John Cotton were living actors in the drama of their times; Cotton Mather was little more than a stereotyped imitator. In the last analysis the New England theocracy fell because it tried to crystallize the Puritan spirit of the early seventeenth century, while the tide of a new civilization swept over and past them.

Vernon Louis Parrington:

THE TWILIGHT OF THE OLIGARCHY

COMMON report has long made out Puritan New England to have been the native seat and germinal source of such ideals and institutions as have come to be regarded as traditionally American. Any critical study of the American mind, therefore, may conveniently seek its beginnings in the colonies clustered about Massachusetts Bay, and will inquire into the causes of the pronounced singularity of temper and purpose that marked off the New England settlements from those to the south, creating a distinctive New England character, and disciplining it for later conquests that were to set a stamp on American life. The course of its somewhat singular development would seem from the first to have been determined by an interweaving of idealism and economics — by the substantial body of thought and customs and institutions brought from the old home, slowly modified by new ways of life developing under the silent pressure of a freer environment. Of these new ways, the first in creative influence was probably the freehold tenure landholdings, put in effect at the beginning and retained unmodified for

From *Main Currents in American Thought,* Volume I, by Vernon Louis Parrington. Copyright 1927, 1930, by Harcourt, Brace and Company, Inc.

generations; and the second was the development of a mercantile spirit that resulted from the sterility of the Massachusetts soil, which encouraged the ambitious to seek wealth in more profitable ways than tilling barren acres. From these sources emerged the two chief classes of New England: the yeomanry, a body of democratic freeholders who constituted the rank and file of the people, and the gentry, a group of capable merchants who dominated the commonwealth from early days to the rise of industrialism. And it was the interweaving of the aims and purposes of these acquisitive yeomen and gentry — harmonious for the most part on the surface, yet driving in different directions — with the ideal of a theocracy and the inhibitions of Puritan dogma, that constitutes the pattern of life to be dealt with here. The Puritan and the Yankee were the two halves of the New England whole, and to overlook or underestimate the contributions of either to the common life is grossly to misinterpret the spirit and character of primitive New England. The Puritan was a contribution of the old world, created by the rugged idealism of the English Reformation; the Yankee was a product of native conditions, created by a practical economics.

* * *

The far-reaching liberalisms implicit in the rejection of a hierarchical organization of the church were to discover no allies in the major premises of the system of theology accepted generally by the English Puritans, and by them transported to New England. Calvinism was no friend of equalitarianism. It was rooted too deeply in the Old Testament for that, was too rigidly aristocratic. It saw too little good in human nature to trust the multitude of the unregenerate;

and this lack of faith was to entail grave consequences upon the development of New England. That the immigrant Puritans brought in their intellectual luggage the system of Calvin rather than of Luther must be reckoned a misfortune, out of which flowed many of the bickerings and much of the intolerance that left a stain on the pages of early New England history.

Two divergent systems of theology, it will be remembered, were spreading through northern Europe during the years of the Reformation, systems that inevitably differentiated in consequence of certain variations of emphasis in the teachings of Luther and Calvin. Both thinkers accepted the adequacy of the Scriptures to all temporal needs, but Luther was at once more mystical and more practical than Calvin, deriving his inspiration chiefly from the New Testament, discovering the creative source of the Christian life in the spiritual union of the soul with Christ, and inclining to tolerance of differences of opinion amongst believers; whereas Calvin was ardently Hebraic, exalting righteousness above love, seeking the law in the Old Testament and laying emphasis on an authoritarian system. The one was implicitly individualistic, the other hierarchical in creative influence. The teachings of Luther, erected on the major principle of justification by faith, conducted straight to political liberty, and he refused to compromise or turn away from pursuing the direct path. If one accepts the doctrine of the priesthood of all believers, one can scarcely refrain from following Luther in his conception of Christian liberty. If the mystical union of the soul with Christ has superseded all lesser loyalties by a higher and more sacred, the enjoyment of spiritual freedom must be reckoned the inalienable right of every child of God. Neither the political state nor the official hierarchy can justly coerce the individual conscience. "One thing and one thing only," said Luther in his *Treatise on Christian Liberty*, "is necessary for Christian life, righteousness and liberty." And from this he deduced the conclusion that "neither pope nor bishop nor any other man has the right to impose a single syllable of law upon a Christian man without his consent; and if he does, it is done in the spirit of tyranny."[1] Clearly, this is the spirit of uncompromising individualism that would eventually espouse the principle of democracy in church and state; and it was their native sympathy with such liberalism that led the radical Separatists to turn more naturally to Luther than to Calvin. Many of the differences that set Roger Williams so greatly apart from the New England brethren must be traced to the Lutheran origins of this thinking.

There was scant room in the rigid system of John Calvin for such Christian liberty. The Genevan thinker was a logician rather than a philosopher, a rigorous system-maker and dogmatist who knotted every argument and tied every strand securely into its fellow, till there was no escape from the net unless one broke through the mesh. To the formalist who demanded an exact system, and to the timid who feared free speculation, the logical consistency of Calvinism made irresistible appeal; and this perhaps suffices to explain its extraordinary hold on the rank and file of middle-class English Presbyterians. More original minds might break with it — men like Richard Hooker and Roger Williams and Vane and Milton — but academic thinkers and schoolmen, men whom the free spaces of thought frightened and who felt safe only

behind secure fences, theologians like John Cotton and his fellows, made a virtue of necessity and fell to declaiming on the excellence of those chains wherewith they were bound. How narrow and cold was their prison they seem never to have realized; but that fact only aggravated the misfortunes that New England was to suffer from the spiritual guidance of such teachers. In seeking for an explanation of the unhappy union of a reactionary theology and a revolutionary political theory, Harriet Beecher Stowe suggested in *Poganuc People* that the Puritan immigrants were the children of two different centuries; that from the sixteenth century they got their theology, and from the seventeenth their politics, with the result that an older absolutism dogma snuggled down side by side in their minds with a later democratic conception of the state and society. In England the potential hostility between Calvinist dogma and individual freedom was perceived by the more liberal Separatists, but in America it was not till the rise of the Revolutionary disputes of the next century that Calvinism was discovered to be the foe of democratic liberalism and was finally rejected. It is a fruitful suggestion, and in its major contention that the liberalisms implicit in the Puritan revolution were ill served by a reactionary theology, it is certainly in harmony with the facts.

That Calvinism in its primary assumptions was a composite of oriental despotism and sixteenth-century monarchism, modified by the medieval conception of a city-state, is clear enough today to anyone who will take the trouble to translate dogma into political terms. In recasting the framework of the old theology, Calvin accepted as a sovereign conception the idea of God as arbitrary and absolute will — an august *Rex regum* whose authority is universal and uncon-

[1] See "The Babylonian Captivity," in *Works*, Vol. II, p. 233 (Philadelphia, 1915).

ditioned; and this conception he invested with Hebraic borrowings from the Old Testament. . . .

From this cosmic absolutism, that conceived of God as the stable Will sustaining the universe, binding together what otherwise would fly asunder, two important corollaries were derived: the universality of the moral law, and the necessity of divine judgment. From the former flowed that curious association of God's will with natural causes which induced Cotton Mather, when suffering from toothache, to inquire what sin he had committed with his teeth, and which left no free spaces or non-moral impulses in the lives of men. From the latter flowed the doctrine of theological determinism. If time is embedded in the eternity of God's mind, if to Him past and future are here and now, foreknowledge is an inevitable divine attribute, and predestination is only a finite way of expressing God's understanding of how human fate works itself out. Ally this doctrine of determinism with the Biblical account of the fall of man, and the doctrine of the elect becomes the theological complement of the class prejudices of the times. Bred up in the current aristocratic contempt for the sodden mass of the people, Calvinist theologians easily came to regard them as stupid, sensual, veritable children of Adam, born to sin and heirs of damnation. Only the elect shall be saved. That there was a remnant in Israel whom God had chosen, Isaiah had long before pointed out; and the doctrine of the remnant was confirmed for Calvinism by the sinful herd whose daily actions testified to their lost estate.

According to such a theology, the individual clearly is in no effective sense a free soul. There is no room for the conception of human perfectibility. The heritage of natural freedom was long since cast away by the common forefather; and because of the pre-natal sin which this act entailed on all mankind, the natural man is shut away eternally from communion with God. He is no better than an oriental serf at the mercy of a Sovereign Will that is implacable, inscrutable, the ruler of a universe predetermined in all its parts and members from the foundation of the earth. Except for the saving grace of divine election, which no human righteousness can purchase, all must go down to the everlasting damnation that awaits the sons of Adam. In the eyes of such a philosophy it is sheer impertinence to talk of the dignity and worth of the individual soul. Men are no other than the worms of the dust. The boon of eternal life is not included in God's enumeration of natural rights; it is a special grant from the Lord of the universe who is pleased to smile on whom he is pleased to smile. In the hard words of Paul, "Therefore hath he mercy on whom he will have mercy, and whom he will he hardeneth." And those on whom he hath had mercy are his Saints, and they are gathered into his church, as the free city-states had risen out of the muck of medieval despotism. They are the stewards of his righteousness and are called to the great work of rulership on earth that God's will may be done and righteousness may prevail over iniquity.

It was an ambitious program, and so long as the Presbyterian party maintained its ascendency in England it endeavored to thrust its Calvinism down every throat, no matter how unwelcome; but with the passing of power from its hands, and the growth of a common-sense spirit of toleration, Calvinistic dogma lost its authority and the minds of Englishmen turned to more humane philosophies. In New England, on the other hand, by virtue of a rigid suppression of free inquiry, Calvinism long lingered out a harsh existence, grotesque and illiberal to the last. In banishing the Antinomians and Separatists and Quakers, the Massachusetts magistrates cast out the spirit of liberalism from the household of the Saints.

* * *

It is not pleasant to linger in the drab later years of a century that in its prime had known able men and accomplished notable things. A world that accepted Michael Wigglesworth for its poet, and accounted Cotton Mather its most distinguished man of letters, had certainly backslidden in the ways of culture. The final harvest of the theocracy must be reckoned somewhat scanty. English Independency had been the robust and rebellious child of a great age; New England Puritanism was the stunted offspring of a petty environment. With the passing of the emigrant generation, a narrow provincialism settled upon the commonwealth of Massachusetts Bay. Not a single notable book appeared; scarcely a single generous figure emerged from the primitive background. A thin soil and the law of Moses created a capable but ungainly race, prosaic and niggardly. Their very speech lost much of the native English beauty that had come down from medieval times. The clean and expressive idiom that Bunyan caught from the lips of English villagers, with its echoes of a more spontaneous life before the Puritan middle class had substituted asceticism for beauty, grew thinner and more meager, its bright homespun dyes subdued to a dun butternut. The town records which in the first years had been set down in dignified and adequate phrase became increasingly crabbed and illiterate, laboriously composed by plain men to whom spelling had become a lost art. The horizons of life in New England were contracting to a narrow round of chores and sermons. "When I first saw the Lieut. Governor," Sewall remarked of Stoughton, "He was Carting Ears of Corn from the Uper Barn." The picture suggests the pastoral note, but it suggests much else as well.

Against this incursion of the provincial the church was the single force to be counted on to do battle. The ministers did their best, but it needed abler men than were available to counteract the growing formalism of the times. They might lament that their admonitions fell on unheeding ears, that they preached in vain to a "sermon-proof, gospel-glutted generation"; but the blame must attach in part to the formalism of their appeals. The straw was over-threshed. The common provincialism infected the pulpit as well as the pew, and the creative vigor of the ministry steadily declined. The ground was being prepared for superstition and bigotry. As the belief spread through the New England villages that the end of the world would fall on the end of the century, men's thoughts naturally ran much on the demonology that is a logical consequence of the Hebraic dualism, and the most intelligent saw no reason to doubt that "the Evening Wolves will be much abroad, when we are near the Evening of the World." The psychology was being prepared for the witch-mania of Salem, and Cotton Mather was only echoing the common belief when he cried, "An Army of Devils is horribly broke in upon the place which is the *Centre*, and after a sort, the First-born of our *English Settlements*."[2] In this matter, as in so many others, the ministers were no better than their congregations; they were blind leaders of the blind, and they

2 *Wonders of the Invisible World* (Boston, 1693), p. 14.

lent their sanction to the intolerance of the mass judgment. In an environment so stifling, with every unfamiliar idea likely to be seized upon as evidence of the devil's wiles, there was no room for free speculation. A generation under the terror of witchcraft was given over to stark reaction. The Salem outbreak was the logical outcome of the long policy of repression, that had hanged Quakers and destroyed independent thought, in its attempt to imprison the natural man in a straitjacket of Puritan righteousness. Emotions long repressed sometimes find sinister outlets, and the witchcraft madness was only a dramatic aftermath of a generation of repressions and inhibitions.[3]

It was during these unhappy years that power finally slipped from the hands of the oligarchy. With the charter gone, a Royal Governor presiding over the Council, and a property qualification instead of a religious test for suffrage, the old order was broken past mending. The members of the oligarchy still hoped against hope, and under the governorship of Phips they made heroic attempts to bolster up the cause; but the Quebec expedition was so badly muddled as to bring the commonwealth to the verge of ruin, and the Governor and Council wrote to England that God had "spit in our faces."[4] Whether or not that was a correct analysis of the divine reaction to the Quebec fiasco is of no importance today; a good many New Englanders, it would seem, doubted it, and under the pressure of high taxes, a depreciated currency and a great debt, they made their dissatisfaction heard at the royal court. When the English government at last "resolved to settle the Countrey," the

end of the oligarchy was come. The cautious amongst them were for throwing the whole responsibility on the Lord: "the foundations being gone, what can the righteous do?" argued Judge Sewall with shrewd worldly-wisdom. But the ministers would make no compromise with Baal. The tongues of false prophets might seduce the people, but they stood for the old order, fighting a losing fight with righteous zeal. On June 1, 1702, Sewall noted in his diary that he had "much adoe to persuade Mr. Willard to dine with me," the pastor being in a sulk because the civil representatives had taken precedence over the ministers in the procession for proclaiming Queen Anne. But in the end even "good Mr. Willard" was forced to acknowledge that his loyalty was given to a lost cause.

*   *   *

For one who is not a loving student of the unamiable bickerings that clutter the records of early New England, and who does not read them by the gentle light of filial loyalty, it would seem presumptuous to venture into the thorny fields tilled by the Mathers. He is certain to get well scratched, and not at all certain to return with any fruit gathered. The rancors of dead partisanships beset him on every side, and the gossip of old wives' tales fills his ears. He will encounter many a slanderous hearsay, and the authentic documents to which he would naturally turn are often inaccessible, and always inhospitable. The countless tracts, for the most part inconsequential, that issued in an unbroken stream from the tireless Mather pens, consuming all the italics in the printer's case, constitute a veritable *cheval-de-frise* to protect their authors' literary reputations from any Philistine attack; and behind that bristling barricade they have long bidden

---

[3] See Lucien Price, "Witchcraft, Then and Now," in *The Nation*, Vol. CXV, No. 2987.

[4] J. T. Adams, *The Founding of New England* (Boston, 1921), p. 442.

defiance to casual invasion. Only a siege can reduce their stronghold and bring them forth into the clear light of day.

Two generations of Harvard scholarship have essayed the undertaking, but there is still wanting the detached critic who will set the Mathers against an adequate historical background, and appraise them objectively in relation to their times. The Harvard contributions are excellent in their way, but a consciousness of dealing with Harvard worthies would seem to have laid the writers under certain inhibitions. Exposition too easily slides into apologetics. The latest study[5] is a somewhat meticulous defense. It is an extraordinarily painstaking document, that has added to our knowledge of Increase Mather's life and work, but it was unhappily conceived in the dark of the moon, a season congenial to strange quirks of fancy. Some tangle it has cleared away, but fresh obstacles have been added by the intrusion of a thesis to be defended. In consequence, the interpretation of motives is colored by special pleading, and the very necessary inquiry into the sources of those virulent antagonisms that sprang up full-armed in the minister's every footprint is put aside as ungermane to a biography. It is an unfortunate assumption for it puts aside much that is crucial. The rehabilitation becomes too easy and complete. It proves too much. It would have us believe that in spite of all the smoke that gathered about Increase Mather's militant pilgrimage through life, there was never any fire of his kindling; that in spite of all the puddles through which the priestly politician splashed to reach his ends, no spot or stain ever smutched his gown. The contention may be sound,

but it puts credulity to the strain, and unless one has something of a Mather stomach for marvels, one is likely to indulge in the luxury of doubt.

The Mathers were a singularly provocative family, capable, ambitious, certain to have a finger in every pie baking in the theocratic oven. From the emigrant Richard with the great voice, chief architect of the Cambridge Platform, to the provincial Cotton, the family combativeness and love of publicity put their marks on New England history. Of the three generations, certainly Increase Mather was the most generously endowed with capacity for leadership; an able man, practical and assertive, liking to be in the forefront of affairs, not wanting his light hidden under a bushel. An arch-conservative, he justified his ways to his conscience by the excellence of the heritage he strove to conserve. A formalist, he satisfied his intellectual curiosity by extolling the sufficiency of the creed of the fathers. He closed the windows of his mind against the winds of new doctrine, and bounded the fields of speculative inquiry by orthodox fences. He was of the succession of John Cotton rather than Thomas Hooker, a priestly theocrat, though never a shuffler like Cotton, less troubled by free inquiry, less by the intellectual. All his life he was inhibited from bold speculation by his personal loyalties and interests. As a beneficiary of things as they were, certain to lose in prestige and power with any relaxing of the theocracy, it would be asking too much of human nature to expect him to question the sufficiency of the established system of which he was the most distinguished representative. Not to have approved it would have been to repudiate his habitual way of thinking, his deepest prejudices, his strongest convictions. He had

5 Kenneth B. Burdock, *Increase Mather, The Foremost American Puritan* (Harvard University Press, 1925; with bibliography).

been molded and shaped by the theocracy; it was the very marrow of his bones; as well demand that pig iron turn molten again after it comes from the matrix. The ore of which he was fashioned was excellent, but once molded it was rigid; there would be no return to fluidity. And so determined by every impact of environment, by every appeal of loyalty, and by a very natural ambition, Increase Mather became a stout upholder of the traditional order, a staunch old Puritan Tory of the theocratic line. How could any promptings of liberalism find nourishment in such a mind?[6] Why should one expect to find in the works of such a man the seeds of new systems of thought or more generous institutions? He was the outstanding figure of the theocracy in the days of its overthrow, but intellectually he was not worthy to unloose the shoe-strings of Roger Williams.

In his professional capacity, Increase Mather was the priest rather than the theologian, a pastor of the flock, an expounder of the creed, rather than a seeker after new light. As a minister his mind was circumscribed by the thinking of John Calvin. He learned nothing from Luther, and was bitterly hostile to those phases of Independency that embodied the more generous Lutheran principles. No man was by temperament better fitted to embrace the coercive spirit of the Genevan discipline. Strong-willed and ascetic, he discovered in discipline the chief end for which the children of Adam are created. A profound admirer of the close-knit Genevan system, he was a Presbyterian in spirit, a man after Calvin's own heart, who clung to the old coercions in an age that was seeking to throw them off. If he counseled innova-

tion it was in the way of strengthening ministerial authority, never in the way of liberalizing either creed or practice. It was the Congregationalism of the Cambridge Platform, and not that of early Plymouth, that he upheld; and to strengthen that order he turned earnestly to the practical work of Presbyterianizing. He was the prime mover in summoning the synod of 1679–80, requested by the Court to consider amongst other things what "may appear necessary for the preventing schisms, haeresies, prophaneness, & the establishment of the churches in one faith & order of the gospell,"[7] and the chief suggestions of the body, of which he was the conspicuous leader, were a return to a stricter discipline, and a strengthening of the passage in the Savoy Confession of faith — adopted by the synod — by borrowings from the Westminster Confession, which "more positively set forth the authority of the state in doctrinal questions."[8]

In 1691, while in London, Mather had been active in the work of uniting the Presbyterian and Congregational churches of England, under articles that would seem to have been more Presbyterian than Congregational; and in 1705, following the curiously spiteful controversy over the Brattle Street Church he joined vigorously in the proposed work of rejuvenating the New England system by engrafting further shoots from the Presbyterian stock. One of these grafts from the London agreement — the principle of licensing ministerial candidates by the association of ministers, thereby effectively preventing the intrusion of un-

---

[6] Compare Murdock, *Increase Mather*, pp. 394–395.

[7] Quoted in W. Walker, *A History of Congregational Churches in the United States* (New York, 1900), p. 187.

[8] *Ibid.*, p. 190. His biographer has overlooked the significance of this. See Murdock, *Increase Mather*, p. 151.

desired members — established itself on the Congregational system; but another — the principle of associational control of the several churches — was blighted by the attack of John Wise.[9] What this desired consolidation of power in the hands of the ministers implied, is suggested by the terms of the Cambridge Platform, which asserted that "the work & duty of the people is expressed in the phrase of obeying their Elders," and that they may not "speak in church, before they have leave from the elders: nor continue so doing, when they require silence, nor may they oppose nor contradict the judgment or sentence of the Elders, without sufficient & weighty cause."[10] Recalling that the elders of a church had been reduced in number to the single minister, one may perhaps venture to suggest that a man ardently working to strengthen the hands of the ministerial oligarchy by further Presbyterianizing was no friend to Separatist-Congregationalism, nor one in whom the spirit of humility would work any lessening of the authority of the Lord's stewards.[11]

In his conception of toleration Mather followed naturally in the footsteps of John Cotton. He would tolerate all views that were not in error, but his criteria of truth were so far from catholic as to lead him into constant and vehement attack upon other sects. As a responsible leader he was careful to clothe his attacks with generous professions; but he never stepped forward to uphold the right of free thought, or to dissuade his brethren from heresy-baiting. His biographer is greatly impressed by the minister's professions, and takes them at somewhat more than face value, forgetting the ancient saying that by the fruits of men's lives they shall be known. Casuistry is useful for purposes of defense, and a skillful apologist can explain away much; but the spirit of toleration revealed in the following passages was certainly no child of liberalism:

The "Anabaptists" had given trouble in New England. They had installed as minister a man excommunicated from the Congregational church, and, when their meeting-house was closed to them, they persisted in assembling publicly before its barred doors rather than worship unmolested in a private house. To Mather these were attacks upon the true faith, and manifest disturbance of the civil peace. Naturally there is some acidity in his strictures on the "blasted Error" of "Antipedobaptism." . . . He denounces Baptists roundly enough, points to their kinship with the turbulent Anabaptists in Europe, and writes: "Are they not generally of a bad Spirit? Bitter enemies to the Lords most eminent Servants? yea, to the faithfull Ambassadors, spitting the cruel venome of Asps against them."

He then concludes: "Nor is the modern reader likely to disagree" with the apology by President Oakes, who wrote in an introduction to Mather's screed:

It is sufficiently known to those that know the Author, that he is none of the Ishmaels of the times, that have their hand against every man and love to be taking a Dog by the Ears . . . or to be dabling in the waters of strife. . . . They that know his Doctrine and manner of life, cannot but know that the life of his Spirit is in the things of prac-

[9] His biographer has somewhat slurred his account of the "Proposals." See p. 282. But his justification is worth noting: "If the original brand of Puritan piety was worth saving, and Mather believed it was, an oligarchic church government was the only means of securing it in an age when men were inclined to change their religious ideas as they changed their thought on other affairs."

[10] W. Walker, *A History of Congregational Churches, etc.*, p. 205.

[11] Compare Murdock, *Increase Mather*, pp. 361–363.

tical Divinity, and the great Design of his ministry is to promote the power and practice of piety in the greatest instances. . . . I dare undertake . . . his design . . . is not to traduce . . . those that are otherwise minded, or expose them to severities & sufferings on the bare account of their opinion.[12]

From these curious passages the unsympathetic realist is likely to draw the conclusions that the spirit of mutual admiration came to early birth in New England, and that it makes a vast difference whose ox is gored. Something of the same casuistry is employed to explain away Increase Mather's unhappy part in the witchcraft mess.[13] The whole matter is involved and rendered difficult by guilty consciences and the need to save reputations, and perhaps the facts are not to be got at; yet it is only another instance to show how quickly candor flies out at the window when a Mather comes in at the door. One may make much or little of the son's statement that Increase grew more tolerant in his later years; it would seem at best to have been only the difference between black and dark gray. A dominating man does not take kindly to differences of counsel. Increase Mather was a stout upholder of the law and order in the shaping of which he had a hand, but he looked with no friendly eye on the architects of a different order; and the bitterness of his later years was the natural consequence of a strong, proud, ambitious man, thwarted in his dearest projects.

If he contributed nothing to a more liberal theology or church organization, it is idle to expect him to have contributed to political speculation. As a leader of the theocracy he meddled much in practical politics, but it would seem that he was quite unread in the political philosophers and wholly ignorant of major principles. The great English liberals of Commonwealth times and later left him untouched. He bought and read many books, but almost none of a political nature.[14] Hobbes, Harrington, Sidney, Milton, Filmer, Locke, were as much out of his intellectual ken as were the speculations of Roger Williams. Interest in political theory had ceased in Massachusetts with the banishment of the great Independent, and the principles of liberal thinkers like Harrington and Milton would have awakened little sympathy in so stalwart a theocrat as Increase Mather. He was a practical man, an administrator and mentor, a stern *castigator morum* to the commonwealth, and as a college president he had been trained in a school little notable for its sympathetic consideration of the views of subordinates. He got on ill with his Harvard tutors, and one of the unseemliest squabbles of his later years grew out of the bitterness sowed between a "strong" administrator and his teaching staff.[15] A man accounted less pious, concerned with ends more patently worldly, might well be reckoned dictatorial and domineering; but Puritan righteousness, perhaps, is not to be judged by profane standards, nor the same severity of judgment applied to politicians laboring in the theocratic vineyard, that is applied to the common breed.

Perhaps the happiest years of Increase Mather's arduous life were those spent in London as agent of the theocratic party to secure such terms as he could for the settlement of New England. It was a congenial task and a congenial field. His

---

[12] Murdock, *Increase Mather*, pp. 138–139.

[13] See pp. 294–295, where he seeks unsuccessfully to refute the position taken by J. T. Adams.

[14] See Murdock, *Increase Mather*, pp. 125–127.

[15] "The Brattle-Street Church Controversy," for which see *ibid.*, pp. 258 ff.

love of diplomacy and his fondness for England were both gratified. He mingled there on terms of equality with the intellectual leaders of English Nonconformity, and matched his wit with men high in station. He proved himself a skillful manager, but the threads were too tangled for any Puritan diplomat to smoothe out, and he fell short of his hopes. The terms of the charter as finally drafted satisfied few of the Boston theocrats, and his nomination of Sir William Phips for Governor was certainly ill-judged. Sir William had been converted to the true faith by Increase himself and was reckoned by him a chosen vessel of the Lord; but he turned out to be no better than a cracked pot, and with the coming of Dudley the political influence of Increase Mather was finally broken. He was maneuvered out of his position as president of Harvard and later suffered the mortification of seeing the post fall into the hands of Leverett, the old tutor now become an influential politician, with whom he had been bitterly at outs. "Doubtless there is not any government in the world," he wrote, "that has been laid under greater obligations by a greater man than this government has been by me. Nevertheless I have received more discouragement in the work of the Lord, by those in government, than by all the men in the world besides. Let not my children put too much confidence in men."[16] It is not pleasant to be ousted from one's position by politicians, and if one is certain that the slight intended for the servant falls on the Master, it is scarcely to be borne. If waves of black pessimism swept over him in those unhappy later years when his ambitions were hopelessly frustrated, there was provocation enough. He had outlived his

age and the ablest of the native-born theocrats had become a byword and a mocking amongst the profane of Boston.

Not a great man, as the world reckons greatness, Increase Mather may scarcely be accounted a great Puritan. As a theologian he was wanting in speculative vigor, and as a pastor he was wanting in self-denying love. It is not necessary to set him over against Roger Williams or Jonathan Edwards or William Ellery Channing, to reveal his intellectual and spiritual shortcomings. One has only to place him beside so rugged and honest a Puritan as Samuel Hopkins, who in true Christian humility, utterly regardless of his own fame, gave his life to theology and the care of the poor and the outcast, to realize how conventional a soul was Increase Mather, how incurious intellectually, how ambitious and self-seeking. Men loved Samuel Hopkins even though they might vigorously reject his doctrine, as they loved Roger Williams and Ellery Channing; but few seem to have loved Increase Mather. One might respect his abilities, but he was too austerely forbidding to like, too overbearing to awaken the spirit of good will. Ideas in the abstract held no interest for him. His biographer has happily recalled Mather's forgotten interest in scientific inquiry, and for this slight relief from the intolerable drab of his life-story one may be grateful. Yet one must not build too high on an insubstantial foundation. In the England that Mather loved, and toward which he was strongly drawn — hoping that opportunity would offer for a pulpit there — pottering over natural philosophy had become a mark of distinction, and a man so envious of repute would have wished to approve himself to those whom he admired. Though he lived in Boston he would not have it thought that he was provincial.

---

16 *Ibid.*, pp. 373–4, note.

Of the miscellaneous literary output that flowed from his pen in an abundant stream, little need be said. It is of concern only to minute historians of the local. That he was master of an excellent prose style, clear and straightforward, is sufficiently evident; if his matter had been so good, his legitimate fame would have been far greater. The work on which his reputation largely rests is *An Essay for the Recording of Illustrious Providences*, printed at Boston and London in 1684, and twice reissued in the nineteenth century under the title *Remarkable Providences*. It is an amusing book of old wives' tales, not singular at all for the times, but characteristic rather; an expression of the naïveté that crops out in Winthrop's *History of New England*, and other writings of the emigrant generation, but now become a fashion amongst the lesser lights of the Royal Academy and English Nonconformists. It suited to a nicety the Mather love of marvels, and Increase constituted himself a generous repository of all the chimney-corner tales of the countryside. To call such a book "a scientific and historical recording of phenomena observed in New England," as his biographer has done, is to gall the back of a thesis with hard riding.[17] In one chapter only does Mather suggest the spirit of scientific inquiry; four out of the twelve deal with witchcraft and kindred topics; and the rest are made up of such instances of divine providence as great fish jumping out of the sea into the boats of starving sailors adrift, of the freaks played by lightning and tornadoes, and of God's punishments on wicked Quakers. At the time it was a harmless enough book, but in the light of after developments it was scarcely so harmless. The emphasis laid

upon witchcraft was an unfortunate, if unconsidered, influence in preparing the psychology of New England for the Salem outbreak, and the minister later reaped a bitter harvest from it.

"Not many years ago," he wrote in the preface to *Illustrious Providences*, "I *lost* (and that's an afflictive *loss* indeed!) several moneths from study by sickness. Let every God-fearing reader joyn with me in prayer, that I may be enabled to redeem the time, and (in all ways wherein I am capable) to serve my generation." That Increase Mather sincerely desired to serve his generation according to his lights, none may deny. His labors were appalling, his reputation was great, and when he died the light of the old churches went out. The spirit of Presbyterianism went to its grave in New England, and not till a hundred years later did the new light — which was no other than primitive English Independency — shine out in the life and work of William Ellery Channing. After two centuries Unitarianism recovered for the Massachusetts churches the spirit of early Separatism that had been lost since the days of the Cambridge Platform. Channing finally uprooted the vine that Increase Mather had so laboriously tended.

Of the unpopularity that gathered about the name of Mather after the fall of the theocracy, the larger portion fell to the lot of the son, the eccentricities of whose character made him peculiarly vulnerable to attack. In his youth the spoiled child of Boston, in middle life he was petulant and irritable, inclined to sulk when his will was crossed. In the career of no other New England Puritan is the inquisitorial pettiness of the Genevan system of theology and discipline revealed so disagreeably. The heroic qualities of an earlier age had atrophied

[17] *Ibid.*, p. 170.

in an atmosphere of formalism, and Boston Calvinism of the year 1690 had become a grotesque caricature of a system that in its vigor had defied the power of Rome and laid kingdoms as its feet. Embodied in Cotton Mather it was garrulous, meddlesome, scolding, an echo of dead voices, a shadow of forgotten realities. The common provincialism had laid its blight upon it. The horizons of the New England imagination grew narrow, and Puritan anthropomorphism unconsciously reduced the God of the Hebrew prophets to the compass of a village priest, clothed in stock and gown, and endowed with the intellect of a parish beadle. In the egocentric universe wherein Cotton Mather lived and labored the cosmos had shrunk to the narrow bounds of a Puritan commonwealth, whereof Boston was the capital and the prosperity of the North Church the special and particular object of divine concern. The mind of Increase Mather had been enlarged by contact with English life; the mind of the son was dwarfed by a village world.

Cotton Mather is an attractive subject for the psychoanalyst. Intensely emotional, high-strung and nervous, he was oversexed and overwrought, subject to ecstatic exaltations and, especially during his celibate years, given to seeing visions. In the carefully edited *Diary* which he left for the edification of his natural and spiritual children, at the beginning of his twenty-third year, is an apologetic entry — *"Cum Relego, Scripsisse Pudet!"* — that Professor Wendell has put into English thus:

A strange and memorable thing. After outpourings of prayer, with the utmost fervor and fasting, there appeared an Angel, whose face shone like the noonday sun. His features were as those of a man, and beardless; his head was encircled by a splendid tiara; on his shoulders were wings; his garments were white and shining; his robe reached to his ankles; and about his loins was a belt not unlike the girdles of the peoples of the East. And this Angel said that he was sent by the Lord Jesus to bear a clear answer to the prayers of a certain youth, and to bear back his words in reply. Many things this Angel said which it is not fit should be set down here. But among other things not to be forgotten he declared that the fate of this youth should be to find full expression for what in him was best; ... And in particular this Angel spoke of the influence his branches should have, and of the books this youth should write and publish, not only in America but in Europe. And he added certain special prophecies of the great works this youth should do for the Church of Christ in the revolutions that are now at hand. Lord Jesus! What is the meaning of this marvel? From the wiles of the Devil, I beseech thee, deliver and defend Thy most unworthy servant.[18]

The passage throws a good deal of light on the psychology of Cotton Mather. Such visions were clearly the result of abnormal stimuli, acting on a neurotic temperament. From both sides of his family he inherited a tense nervous system that was aggravated by precocity and an unnatural regimen. The inevitable result was a hothouse plant of Puritan forcing. His religious exaltation flowered from the root of egoism. His vanity was cosmic. He esteemed himself a beacon set on a hill, a divine torch which the very hand of God had lighted. The success or failure of God's plan for New England, he believed, rested on his shoulders; and with such heavy responsibilities devolved upon him he was driven, hot-haste, by the prick of urgency. The king's business requireth

[18] Barrett Wendell, *Cotton Mather, Puritan Priest* (New York, 1891; Harvard University Press, 1925), p. 64.

haste. The work of the Lord cannot wait upon sluggards. "O then *To work* as fast as you can," he wrote in the *Magnalia*, "and of soul-work and church-work as much as ever you can. Say to all *Hindrances* . . . 'You'll excuse me if I ask you to be short with me, for my work is great and my time is but little.' " And so with an amazing activity that was little short of neurosis, he gave himself over to the great business of managing the affairs of New England in accordance with God's will.

In undertaking so difficult a job, he frequently came into conflict with other interpreters of God's plan for New England, and partisan venom gathered about him wherever he passed. Tact was never a Mather virtue, and Cotton made two enemies to his father's one. His quarrels trod on each other's heels, and a downright vindictiveness breathes through his private records of them. He railed at whoever disagreed with him, and imputed silly or malignant motives. The pages of his diary are filled with epithets that he flung privately at his enemies; one marvels that so many in the little town of Boston could be singled out as "strangely and fiercely possessed of the Devil." Robert Calef, whose *More Wonders of the Invisible World* was an inconvenient reply to his *Wonders of the Invisible World*, was set down as "a very wicked sort of a Sadducee in this Town, raking together a crue of Libels . . . an abominable Bundle of Lies, written on purpose, with a Quil under a special Energy and Management of Satan, to damnify my precious Opportunities of Glorifying my Lord Jesus Christ."[19] When an anti-Mather group of Cambridge men set up the Brattle Street Church, and invited Benjamin Colman, who had received Presbyterian ordination in England, by way of reply to the Mather group, to become their pastor, Cotton wrote in his diary:

A Company of Head-strong Men in the Town, the cheef of whom, are full of malignity to the Holy Waye of our Churches, have built in this Town, another Meeting-house. To delude many better-meaning Men in their own Company, and the Churches in the Neighbourhood, they past a Vote . . . that they would not vary from the Practice of these Churches, except in one little Particular. . . . But a young Man, born and bred here, and hence gone for England, is now returned hither, at their Invitation, equip'd with an *Ordination*, to qualify him, for all that is intended.

On his "returning and arriving here," these fallacious People" gave themselves over, in short, to "Their violent and impetuous Lusts, to carry on the Apostasy," and Cotton Mather prayed God to make him an instrument to defeat the "Designs that Satan may have in the Enterprise."[20] Similar passages of extravagant abuse of men so wicked as to disagree with him flowed from his pen in copious abundance. Although he constantly prayed that his daily life might be "a trembling walk with God," he was clearly a difficult fellow to get on with; and in the opinion of many he was justly described by a contemporary, as a "malecontent priest," consumed with an "Hereditary rancour" that made him "everlastingly opposite" to every will but his own.

The diary of Cotton Mather is a treasure-trove to the abnormal psychologist. The thing would be inconceivable if the record were not in print. What a crooked and diseased mind lay back of those eyes that were forever spying out occasions to magnify self! He grovels in proud self-

---

[19] *Diary*, Vol. I, p. 271.

[20] *Ibid.*, pp. 325–326.

abasement. He distorts the most obvious reality. His mind is clogged with the strangest miscellany of truth and marvel. He labors to acquire the possessions of a scholar, but he listens to old wives' tales with greedy avidity. In all his mental processes the solidest fact falls into fantastic perspective. He was earnest to do good, he labored to put into effect hundreds of "Good devices," but he walked always in his own shadow. His egoism blots out charity and even the divine mercy. Consider his account of an "execution sermon" preached to a nameless girl condemned for killing her natural child, and the light it throws on both minister and congregation:

The Execution of the miserable Malefactor, was ordered for to have been the last Week, upon the Lecture of another. I wondred then what would become of my *Particular* Faith, of her condition being so ordered in the Providence of God, that it should furnish me, with a *special Opportunity* to glorify Him. While I was entirely resigning to the wisdome of Heaven all such Matters, the Judges, wholly without my seeking, altered and allow'd her Execution to fall on the Day of *my Lecture*. The *General Court* then sitting, ordered the Lecture to bee held in a larger and a stronger House, than that *old* one, where 'tis usually kept. For my own part, I was weak, and faint, and spent; but I humbly gave myself up to the *Spirit* of my Heavenly Lord and Hee assured mee, that Hee would send His good Angel to strengthen mee. The greatest Assembly, ever in this Countrey preach'd unto, was now come together; It may bee four or five thousand Souls. I could not gett unto the *Pulpit*, but by climbing over *Pues* and *Heads:* and there the Spirit of my dearest Lord came upon mee. I preached with a more than ordinary Assistance, and enlarged, and uttered the most awakening Things, for near two hours together. My Strength and Voice failed not; but when it was near failing, a silent Look to Heaven strangely renew'd it. In the whole I found Prayer answered and Hope exceeded, and Faith encouraged, and the Lord using *mee*, the vilest in all that great Assembly, to glorify Him. Oh! what shall I render to the Lord! [21]

Straightway thereafter, he rendered the Lord another characteristic service. No sooner was the girl hanged — for whose safekeeping no good angel seems to have been available after the minister had bespoken his — than he hastened to the printer to arrange for printing the sermon, and "annexed thereunto, an History of Criminals executed in this Land, and effectually, an Account of their dying Speeches, and of my own Discourses with them in their last Hours. . . . I entitled the Book, PILLARS OF SALT." Clearly this was the time to peddle his wares, when all Boston was talking of the great event; and with a nose for publicity as keen as Defoe's, he flung together a jumble of material, and trusted to its timeliness to sell. Some such origin, no doubt, accounts for a good many of the small library of titles that bore his name, an output that seems to have justified the angelic prophecy of "the books this youth should write and publish." With a very lust for printer's ink, he padded his bibliography like a college professor seeking promotion; but in spite of all the prayers poured out in behalf of them, they would seem for the most part to have been little more than tuppenny tracts, stuffed with a sodden morality, that not even an angel could make literature of.

Holding so strong a conviction of apostleship, Cotton Mather would certainly play the politician, and quite as certainly blunder and go wrong. Far more than his father he was a bookman,

21 *Diary*, Vol. I, p. 279.

who believed that all knowledge was shut up between pigskin covers. He was as lacking in worldly wisdom as a child, and in his ecstatic contemplation of the marvels wrought by God in primitive New England he never discovered that that older world had passed away. Another age was rising, with other ideals than ecclesiastical, which the three thousand books in his library told him nothing about. He was an anachronism in his own day. Living in an earlier age, when the hierarchy was in its prime, he would have been carried far on the tide of theocratic prestige; a generation later, when lay-power had definitely superseded clerical, he would have taken his place as a stout defender of Tory ways. But at the moment when a critical realignment of parties was under way in Massachusetts; when the villages were becoming democratized and the gentry tory-ized; when even the clergy were dividing — Cotton Mather was a general without an army. He was a primitive Puritan in a Boston that was fast becoming Yankee, and his love for the theocracy grew stronger with every defeat. . . .

It was easy for so reactionary a nature to slide over into the Tory. There was not a grain of liberalism in his make-up. His antipathy to all popular movements was deep-rooted, for he knew no other political philosophy than that of the obsolete theocracy in which he had grown up. He was a bourgeois soul who loved respectability and was jealous of his social position; no fraternizing with the poor and outcast for him, no profitless excursions into the realms of Utopian justice. Though he might play to popular prejudices to serve his political ends, he had scant regard for popular rights. The highest privilege of the New England people, he believed, was the privilege of being ruled by the godly. His real attitude

towards the plain people is revealed in a note by his son, that refers to the days following the overturn of the Andros government:

Upon Discoursing with him of the Affairs he has told me that he always pressed *Peace* and *Love* and *Submission* unto a legal Government, tho' he suffered from some tumultuous People, by doing so; and upon the whole, has asserted unto me his *Innocency* and Freedom from all known Iniquity in that time, but declared his Resolution, from the View he had of the fickle Humors of the Populace, that he would chuse to be concern'd with them as little as possible for the future.[22]

As he grew older and the shadow of failure fell across his life, his bitterness towards a people that had rejected his admonitions is revealed on many a page of his diary. It was a "silly people," a "foolish people," "insignificant lice" — "The cursed clamour of a people strangely and fiercely possessed of the Devil" — "My aged father laies to heart the withdrawal of a vain, proud, foolish people from him in his age" — "It is the Hour of . . . Darkness on this Despicable Town." He could not easily forgive those who had wounded his love of power and lust of adulation, and he was too aloof from the daily life of men to understand the political and social movements of the times, too self-centered to understand his fellow villagers. He possessed none of the sympathetic friendliness that made Samuel Sewall a natural confidant to every one in trouble. He loved the people when they honored and obeyed him, but when they hearkened to other counsels he would fall to scolding like a fishwife. Doubtless he was sincere in thinking he would gladly die to save his people from

22 Wendell, *Cotton Mather, etc.*, p. 82.

their sins, but he had no mind to neighbor with them or humor their wicked love of power. He immured himself so closely within the walls of the old theocratic temple that he never took the trouble to examine the groundsills, and when the rotten timbers gave way and the structure came tumbling about his ears, he was caught unprepared and went down in its ruins.

Happily most of the printed output of Cotton Mather has fallen into the oblivion it deserved. It is barren of ideas, and marred by pedantic mannerisms that submerge the frequent felicities of phrase — old-fashioned on the day it came from the press. "In his *Style*, indeed," wrote his friend Thomas Prince, "he was something singular, and not so agreeable to the Gust of the Age. But like his *manner of speaking*, it was very *emphatical*." Yet he possessed very considerable gifts and under happier circumstances he might have had a notable literary career; but he was the victim of a provincial environment. He was the most widely read man of his generation in America, and one of the few who followed sympathetically the current scientific movement in England. Like old Increase he dabbled in science; he was proud of his membership in the Royal Society, to which he forwarded his characteristic *Curiosa Americana* — a hodgepodge of those marvels in which his generation delighted. It was from an English source that he got the idea of inoculation for smallpox, which he urged upon Boston so insistently that a war of scurrilous pamphlets broke out. He made use of the method in his own family, incurring thereby much stupid abuse and at least one attack of violence. It was an intelligent and courageous experiment, that is not to be forgotten in casting up the accounts of Cotton Mather.

Of his major works two only call for brief consideration: the celebrated *Magnalia Christi Americana; or, The Ecclesiastical History of New England;* and the less known *Wonders of the Invisible World.* The latter is suggestive for the light it throws on the psychology of the witchcraft mania. The fantastic devil-fear, which bit so deeply into the imagination of Puritan New England, has already been commented on. In that common seventeenth-century delusion, Cotton Mather not only ran with the mob, but he came near to outdistancing the most credulous. His speech and writings dripped with devil-talk. The grotesqueries that marked the current marvel-tales crop out nakedly in his writings. "I have set myself," he wrote in the *Diary*, "to countermine the whole Plot of the Devil, against New-England, in every branch of it, as far as one of my *darkness* can comprehend such a *Work* of Darkness." His conviction of the malignant activities of Satan was so vivid, that in delivering a carefully prepared sermon on the *Wiles of the Devil*, he was fain, he tells us, to pause and lift up his eyes and cry "unto the Lord Jesus Christ, that he would rate off Satan," who "all the Time of my Prayer before the Lecture" had "horribly buffeted me" — by inflicting on the fasting priest certain qualms of the stomach. How tremendous he conceived to be the battle over a human soul, he describes thus:

The *Wilderness* through which we are passing to the Promised Land is all over fill'd with Fiery flying serpents. But, blessed be God, none of them have hitherto so fastned upon us as to confound us utterly! All our way to Heaven lies by *Dens of Lions* and the *Mounts of Leopards;* there are incredible Droves of Devils in our way. . . . We are poor travellers in a world which is as well the Devil's Field, as the Devil's *Gaol;* a world in

which every Nook whereof, the Devil is en-
camped with *Bands of Robbers* to pester all
that have their Faces looking Zionward.[23]

In the light of Mather's logic, "That there
is a *Devil*, is a thing Doubted by none
but such as are under the influence of
the Devil," and "God indeed has the
Devil in a *Chain*, but has horribly length-
ened out the Chain," his private com-
ment on the work — that "reviled book"—
becomes comprehensible.

The *Magnalia* is a far more important
work, the repository of a vast miscellany
of information concerning early New
England that his pious zeal saved from
oblivion. It is the *magnum opus* of the
Massachusetts theocracy, the best and
sincerest work that Cotton Mather did.
The theme with which it deals, and
about which he accumulates marvels and
special providences together with historical facts, was the thing which next to
his own fame lay nearest his heart — the
glory of that theocracy which men whom
he accounted foolish and wicked were
seeking to destroy. The purpose of the
book has nowhere been better stated
than by Professor Wendell:

Its true motive was to excite so enthusi-
astic a sympathy with the ideals of the Puritan fathers that, whatever fate might befall
the civil government, their ancestral semi-
nary of learning should remain true to its
colours. . . . The time was come, Cotton
Mather thought, when the history of these
three generations might be critically examined; if this examination should result in
showing that there had lived in New England
an unprecedented proportion of men and
women and children whose earthly existence
had given signs that they were among the
elect, then his book might go far to prove
that the pristine policy of New England had
been especially favoured of the Lord. For

surely the Lord would choose His elect most
eagerly in places where life was conducted
most according to His will.[24]

When old Increase was near the end
of his many years, a friend wrote to ask
if he were still in the land of the living.
"No, Tell him I am going to it," he said
to his son; "this Poor World is the land
of the Dying." The bitter words were
sober truth. The New England of the
dreams of Increase and Cotton Mather
was sick to death from morbid introspec-
tion and ascetic inhibitions; no lancet or
purge known to the Puritan pharmaco-
poeia could save it. Though father and
son walked the streets of Boston at noonday, they were only twilight figures,
communing with ghosts, building with
shadows. They were not unlike a certain
mad woman that Sewall tells of, who
went crying about the town, "My child
is dead within me." The child of Cotton
Mather's hopes had long been dead
within him, only he could not bring himself to acknowledge it. The fruit of the
vine planted by the fathers was still
sweet to him, and when other men complained of its bitterness, and fell to
gathering from other vines, he could only
rail at their perversity. He would not
believe that the grapes were indeed bitter and the vine blighted; that the old
vineyard must be replowed and planted
to fresh stock. All his life he had set
marvels above realities and in the end his
wonder-working providence failed him.
Prayers could not bring back a dead past;
passionate conjurations could not strike
the living waters from the cold granite
of Puritan formalism. A New England
flagellant, a Puritan Brother of the Cross,
he sought comfort in fasts and vigils and
spiritual castigations, and — it is pleasant

[23] *Wonders of the Invisible World*, p. 63.

[24] *Literary History of America*, pp. 48–49.

to learn — in ways far more natural and wholesome. Incredible as it may seem, the following record is authentic, and it falls like a shaft of warm sunshine across the path of the morbid priest: "Augt, 15. [1716]. . . . Now about Dr. C. Mather Fishing in Spy-pond, falls into the Water, the boat being ticklish, but receives no hurt."[25] The restless minister who had fished overmuch in troubled waters, sometimes, it would appear, ventured for perch in Spy Pond.

[25] Sewall, *Diary,* Vol. III, p. 98.

Charles Francis Adams:
MASSACHUSETTS: ITS HISTORIANS
AND ITS HISTORY

THE same anomaly and apparent contradiction runs through the history of Massachusetts during the two centuries which followed the settlement, the same "love of independence and hatred of tyranny" which "saved the country from the yoke of a cruel despotism," and the same "religious servitude" which encouraged superstition, "prolonged the reign of ignorance and stopped the march of society." This, indeed, constitutes to my mind the keynote of Massachusetts, as it did with Buckle of Scotch history and yet, so far as I am aware, a single writer only has even alluded to it, and that one, a writer not to the manor born.[1] In his book entitled *The English in America,* J. A. Doyle remarks that, "The spiritual growth of Massachusetts withered under the shadow of dominant orthodoxy; the colony was only saved from mental atrophy by its vigorous political life"; and he adds of the established church of Massachusetts that while, by forcibly suppressing free speech through the action of the civil magistrates, the church cut the community off from all hopes of intellectual progress, "her rule so long as it endured was a rule of terror, not of love; her ways were never ways of pleasantness, her paths were never peace."[2] As one of its mouthpieces proclaimed, New England Congregationalism "was a speaking Aristocracy in the face of a silent Democracy."[3]

To describe in detail the action and counter-action of these two forces, the vigorous political life on the one side and the shadow of spiritual orthodoxy on the other, would be to re-write the history of Massachusetts. For that there is neither

[1] "Casting aside all but ecclesiastical considerations, the clergy consistently rejected any compromise with the crown which threatened to touch the church. Almost from the first they had recognized that substantial independence was necessary in order to maintain the theocracy." — Brooks Adams, *Emancipation of Massachusetts,* 205.

[2] *The English in America; the Puritan Colonies,* vol. i, pp. 187, 188.

[3] The Rev. Samuel Stone, of Hartford. Quoted in Cotton Mather, *Magnalia Christi Americana,* III, chap. xvi.

present space nor time; nor yet, indeed, occasion. A brief outline will suffice; but that outline must of necessity cover the leading events and the principal characters who figured in those events, through two centuries and a half.

The turning point in the history of early Massachusetts was the Cambridge Synod of September, 1637, the first convocation of the kind ever held in America, that already referred to as "carried on so peaceably, and concluded so comfortably in all love," which succeeded in spreading on its record, as then prevailing in the infant settlement, eighty-two "opinions, some blasphemous, others erroneous and all unsafe," besides "nine unwholesome expressions," the whole mighty mass of which was then incontinently dismissed, in the language of one of the leading divines who figured in that Assembly, "to the devil of hell, from whence they came."

The mere enumeration of this long list of heresies as then somewhere prevailing is strong evidence of intellectual activity in early Massachusetts, an activity which found ready expression through such men as Roger Williams, John Cotton, John Wheelwright and Sir Henry Vane, to say nothing of Mrs. Hutchinson, while the receptive condition of the mental soil is likewise seen in the hold the new opinions took. It was plainly a period of intellectual quickening, a dawn of promise. Of this there can no doubt exist. It was freely acknowledged at the time; it has been stated as one of the conditions of that period by all writers on it since. The body of those who listened to him stood by Roger Williams; and the magistrates drove him away for that reason.[4] Anne Hutchinson so held

the ear of the whole Boston community that she had "some of all sorts and quality, in all places to defend and patronize" her opinions; "some of the magistrates, some gentlemen, some scholars and men of learning, some Burgesses of our General Court, some of our captains and soldiers, some chief men in towns, and some men eminent for religion, parts and wit."[5] These words of a leader of the clerical faction, one of those most active in the work of repression, describe to the life an active-minded, intelligent community quick to receive and ready to assimilate that which is new. Then came the Synod. It was a premonition. It was as if the fresh new sap, the young budding leaves, the possible, incipient flowers had felt the chill of an approaching glacier. And that was exactly what it was; a theological glacier then slowly settled down upon Massachusetts, a glacier lasting through a period of nearly one hundred and fifty years, the single redeeming feature in which was that beneath the chilling and killing superincumbent mass of theology, superstition and intolerance ran the strong, vivifying current of political opposition and life.

That, like most phases of historical development, this was all inevitable, the logical outcome of what had gone before, is to us apparent; but it in no way alters the fact. It was natural that in the mass of self-exiled men who sought refuge in Massachusetts between 1630 and 1637, there should be many of active, inquiring mind. Indeed it could not have been otherwise. On the other hand, the fundamental idea of the settlement was a theocracy, an Israel in the New World, a reproduction of Bible history. A struggle was inevitable, for theocracy was incompatible with mental activity, just as in-

[4] Savage's *Winthrop*, vol. i, p. 175; Cotton's *Answer* (in Publications of Narragansett Club, vol. ii, p. 93).

[5] Thomas Welde, Preface to *Short Story*.

compatible as is superstition with a spirit of investigation and doubt. Mere brute instinct sufficed to make this plain. The struggle took place in 1637 and was as decisive as it was short. The orthodox theological spirit gained an easy and complete ascendency; and the glacial period began. There was no further contest. It was a mere question thereafter of maintaining an undisputed ascendency. . . .

The theologico-glacial period of Massachusetts may, therefore, be considered as lasting from the meeting of the Cambridge Synod in September, 1637, to the agitation over the Writs of Assistance in February, 1761, culminating in what is known as "the Great Awakening" of 1740–5. As a period it was singularly barren, almost inconceivably sombre. It has left behind it a not inconsiderable residuum of printed matter, mainly theological, but of little, if indeed of any literary value. Than this residuum there can, indeed, "be no better proof how fully Puritanism had done its destructive work. Bid the New Englander tell the great things which God had wrought by him and his countrymen, his deep and overpowering faith raised him to noble thoughts, his scriptural learning clothed them in noble language; bring him to a lower range, to the sphere of the disputant, the critic, or the essayist, and all sense of grace, of proportion or humor has vanished."[6] In the mother country that period was a fruitful season, for it began with Milton and closed with Johnson; while Clarendon and Burnet, Dryden, Pope and Goldsmith, Bunyan, Swift, Addison, Steele and Defoe, Locke, Bolingbroke and Newton were included in it. In Massachusetts, of writers or thinkers whose names are still remembered though their works have passed into oblivion, Cotton Mather and Jonathan Edwards can alone be named. They were, indeed, typical of the time, strange products of a period at once provincial and glacial, huge literary boulders deposited by the receding ice.

"The grave humorists, who call themselves historians of philosophy, seem to be at times under the impression that the development of the world has been affected by the last new feat of some great man in the art of logical hairsplitting."[7] In other words, the writer, the thinker, the typical man in philosophy as in every other branch of human development is not a cause, or if a cause at all, only such in a very minor degree, but the conditions of development must be sought in the "environment" as well as in the new expression. "We can only explain the spread of the organism by showing how and why the soil was congenial." Cotton Mather and Jonathan Edwards were the ripe fruit of the theological period of Massachusetts; its outcome was "the Great Awakening." In the writings of the first and in the history of the last that period can best be studied. By its fruits it must be judged!

The strange story of the religious revival which swept over New England about the year 1742 — that frenzied epidemic of superstitious excitement — has been told in sufficient detail by Palfrey.[8] Presently I shall have occasion to refer to it in detail; suffice it now to say that the more its details are studied the more incredible they seem. It was an exaggerated case of mania, at once emotional and devotional, not unlike the similar mania which spread over Europe six

---

[6] Doyle, *The Puritan Colonies*, vol. ii, p. 103.

[7] Stephen, *An Agnostic's Apology*, p. 309.

[8] *History*, vol. v, pp. 3–41.

hundred and fifty years before in the days of Peter the Hermit, though, of course, on a greatly reduced scale. As to the Rev. Cotton Mather and his literary productions, two biographies of this most typical Massachusetts colonial divine have been issued from the press within the last eighteen months. In their pages he can be studied; though to obtain any realizing sense of the man and of the community in which he lived and for which he wrote, recourse must be had to the *Magnalia* itself. Considered purely as a literary character and one of the most prolific of authors, Cotton Mather's career was, in point of time, nearly identical with that of Daniel Defoe; for born two years later than his English contemporary, he died three years earlier, and the *Magnalia* was printed in London at about the same time as that famous tract entitled *The Shortest Way with Dissenters*, which at once elevated Defoe to literary fame and to the pillory. Of Mather it has recently been said that:

He was the last, the most vigorous, and, therefore, the most disagreeable representation of the Fantastic school in literature. . . . The expulsion of the beautiful from thought, from sentiment, from language; a lawless and a merciless fury for the odd, the disorderly, the grotesque, the violent; strained analogies, unexpected images, pedantries, indelicacies, freaks of allusion, monstrosities of phrase; these are the traits of Cotton Mather's writing, even as they are the traits common to that perverse and detestable literary mood that held sway in different countries of Christendom during the sixteenth and seventeenth centuries. Its birthplace was Italy; New England was its grave; Cotton Mather was its last great apostle.[9]

But it is a fact worthy of note that the *Magnalia* stands to-day the one single

[9] Tyler, *American Literature*, vol. ii, pp. 87, 88.

literary landmark in a century and a half of colonial and provincial life, a geological relic of a glacial period, a period which in pure letters produced, so far as Massachusetts was concerned, absolutely nothing else, not a poem, nor an essay, nor a memoir, nor a work of fancy or fiction of which the world has cared to take note. . . .[10]

The pulpit was the intellectual, moral and religious rostrum of early Massachu-

[10] The following, from one of his better literary efforts, are not unfair specimens of Cotton Mather's method of thought and quaintness of expression:
I would be Sollicitous to have my *Children* Expert, not only at *Reading* handsomely, but also at *Writing* a fair Hand. I will then assign them such *Books* to *Read*, as I may judge most agreeable and profitable; obliging them to give me some Account of what they *Read*; but keep a Strict Eye upon them, that they don't Stumble on *the Devils Library*, and poison themselves with foolish *Romances*, or *Novels*, or *Playes*, or *Songs*, or *Jests that are not convenient*. I will set them also, to *Write* out such things, as may be of the greatest Benefit unto them; and they shall have their Blank Books, neatly kept on purpose, to Enter such Passages as I advise them to. I will particularly require them now and then, to *Write* a *Prayer* of their own Composing, and bring it unto me; that so I may discern, what sense they have of their own Everlasting Interests. — *Essays to do Good*, p. 58.
Nero took it very ill, that *Vespasian* Slept, at his *Musick*. It is very much, very much to be Wished, That the Sin of *Sleeping* at *Sermons*, were much more Watch'd against, and more Warn'd against. Your *Sleepy Hearers*, if, alas, the *Catechresis* may be allow'd that calls them *Hearers*, do miserably lose the *Good* of your Ministry; and the *Good* which you might, perhaps, have particularly design'd for them, whom at the Time of your Speaking what you prepar'd for them, you see Siezed with an horrible *Spirit of Slumber* before your Eyes. Will no *Vinegar* help against the *Narcoticks*, that Satan has given to your Poor Eutychus's? Or, Can't you bring that *Civility* into Fashion among your Hearers, to *wake one another?* — *Ibid.*, p. 103.
Speaking of his "thirst for knowledge" as a boy of twelve, Franklin, in his *Autobiography*, refers especially to a "book of De Foe's, called an *Essay on Projects*, and another of Dr. Mather's, called *Essays to do Good*, which perhaps gave me a turn of thinking that had an influence on some of the principal future events of my life."

setts and it is not putting it too strongly to say that the pulpit oratory of that period is one long Jeremiad, an unending, monotonous wail over the degeneracy of the present as compared with the past, over the decay of religious fervor and the neglect of observances, over the apostacies of the people of God. Here, for instance, is a specimen from a discourse entitled *The Glory Departing from New England,* delivered by Increase Mather in 1702:

O New England! New England! Look to it, that the Glory be not removed from thee. For it begins to go. . . . The Glory of the Lord seems to be on the wing. Oh! Tremble for it is going, it is gradually departing. . . . You that are Aged persons, and can remember what New England was Fifty Years ago, that saw these churches in *their first Glory;* Is there not a sad decay and diminution of the Glory? We may weep to think of it. . . . Ancient men, though they bless God for what they *Do* see of His Glory remaining in these Churches, they cannot but mourn when they remember what they *Have* seen, far surpassing what is at present.

But possibly the climax of Cassandra-like ravings was reached by Dr. Increase Mather when in 1696, being then President of this College, he remarked to the students in a discourse delivered in the college-hall:

It is the Judgment of very learned Men, that, in the glorious Times promised to the Church on Earth, *America* will be *Hell.* And, although there is a Number of the Elect of *God* to be born here, I am very afraid, that, in Process of Time, *New England* will be the wofullest place in all *America;* as some other Parts of the World, once famous for Religion, are now the dolefullest on Earth, perfect pictures and emblems of *Hell,* when you see this little Academy fallen to the Ground, then

know it is a terrible Thing, which God is about to bring upon this Land.[11]

The result of this teaching was, of course, a thoroughly morbid general condition, no food pleased the moral palate unless highly seasoned. As a contemporary writer noted, should the people "hear a minister preach in the most evangelical manner upon any moral duty, or recommend the exercise of reason and understanding, they would call him a dry, husky Arminian preacher, and conclude for certain that he was not converted. No sermons please but such as heat the passions, or scare and frighten them. Solid instruction is heathen morality or carnal preaching."[12]

Accordingly in the arid waste of those pulpit deliverances one meets with no occasional gleam of humor or insight, no conception of a spirit of inquiry or observation, no desire to look for a why or a wherefore. The dry husks are fed out, the old straw is thrashed over. Nor did the evil stop here. "Added to all this," it was in Massachusetts as it had been in Europe, "the overwhelming importance attached to theology diverted to it all those intellects which in another condition of society would have been employed in the investigations of science."[13] An utterly false method of reasoning was in vogue, making any real progress impossible. Recurring for an illustration of this once more to Jonathan Edwards, in a sermon of his entitled *Eternity of Hell Torments,* from which I have already quoted, he argues against annihilation in the following way:

The state of the future punishment of the wicked is evidently represented to be a state

[11] *Man knows not his Time,* p. 37.
[12] Quoted by Palfrey, vol. v, p. 37.
[13] Lecky, *Hist. of Rationalism,* vol. i, p. 282.

of existence and sensibility, when it is said, that they shall be cast into a lake of fire and brimstone. How can this expression with any propriety be understood to mean a state of annihilation? Yea, they are expressly said to *have no rest* day or night, but to be *tormented* with fire and brimstone for ever and ever, Rev. xx. 10. But annihilation is a state of *rest*, a state in which not the least *torment* can possibly be suffered. The rich man in hell *lifted up his eyes being in torment*, and saw Abraham afar off, and Lazarus in his bosom, and entered into a particular *conversation* with Abraham; all which proves that he was not annihilated.

This is thoroughly characteristic both of Edwards and of the system of teaching in use during the theologico-glacial period. Nothing could be more deceptive or vicious. Starting from the literal construction of a translated version of a text assumed to be in the original inspired, they argued deductively, with pitiless logic, to conclusions which it was impossible to escape from without, by questioning the premises, incurring a charge of infidelity and atheism. And this system, which by putting a final stop to any intellectual movement, created a universal paralysis, this system had to be slowly outgrown.

But in all this there was nothing new, nothing peculiar to America. Long before, Bacon wrote in England:

Nor should we neglect to observe that Natural Philosophy has, in every age, met with a troublesome and difficult opponent: I mean Superstition, and a blind and immoderate zeal for Religion. . . . In short, you may find all access to any species of Philosophy, however pure, intercepted by the ignorance of Divines. Some, in their simplicity, are apprehensive that a too deep inquiry into Nature may penetrate beyond the proper bounds of decorum, transferring and absurdly applying what is said of sacred Mysteries in Holy Writ against those who pry

into divine secrets, to the mysteries of Nature, which are not forbidden by any prohibition. Others, with more cunning, imagine and consider that if secondary causes be unknown, everything may more easily be referred to the divine hand and wand; a matter as they think, of the greatest consequence to Religion, but which can only really mean that *God wishes to be gratified by means of falsehood.*[14]

And so the great originator of inductive reasoning concluded that "an instauration must be made from the very foundations, if we do not wish to revolve forever in a circle, making only some slight and contemptible progress"; and as it was in England in the beginning of the seventeenth century, so was it in Massachusetts in the middle of the eighteenth century. The world moves slowly. But it does move!

Thus three generations of the children of the soil toiled here in New England painfully across the ever thickening crust of lava which had poured from a volcano, once living but long since extinct; and the only thing the teachers seemed greatly to deplore was the creation of a new soil on the black and desolate waste from which they could anticipate nothing but harvests of poisonous weeds. Superstition and bigotry were thus the trade staples of the educated men of the period. In other words, that people — men and women, old and young, down to the very children in the nursery — were crushed and driven to the verge of insanity, and often over that verge, by a superstitious terror — the terror of what their teachers defined as God's "vindictive justice." If any one doubts this statement, or feels disposed to put it aside as an exaggeration, they have but to turn to Jonathan Edwards's *Faithful Narrative* and Cotton Mather's *Magnalia* and there

[14] *Novum Organum*, I, xxxi, lxxxix.

read the piteous stories of little Phebe Bartlett and little Anne Greenough, each aged five, blighted and driven crazy in their nurseries by fear of death and hell; and for that reason exhibited as prodigies of infant piety![15]

Yet, strange to say, there is even now a generally accepted belief that, somehow or in some way, this degrading parody of religion, this burlesque of philosophy, this system worse than that of Dotheboys Hall, which if in practice upon children today would be indicted by any intelligent commission of lunacy, the belief, I say, prevails that this system in its day subjected the people of Massachusetts to a most useful, though severe discipline, the good results of which their descendants enjoy, though they have themselves fallen away from the strict faith. Nor is this merely a popular belief; it silently pervades the pages of the historian and the moralist. It is needless to say that for any such belief no ground is disclosed by a closer historical research. The Massachusetts of the time prior to 1760 was, it is true, poorer and simpler and more primitive than the Massachusetts of the later period; but that it was morally any better is unsupported by evidence, while it was infinitely less intelligent, less charitable and less cleanly. There is also no more reason to suppose that the terrifying theology then sedulously taught was less an injury to the men, women and children composing the generations which lived prior to 1760 than it would be to those living now. It is, indeed, one of the curious phenomena of man's mental make-up, this implicitly accepted belief that a religious practice or creed which has now become abhorrent, and is recognized as morbid, should once have produced most beneficent results; while on the other hand, it is equally recognized that some Sangrado method of medical treatment, known to be bad now, was equally bad then. The simple fact is that the Calvinistic, orthodox tenets of the seventeenth and eighteenth centuries constituted nothing more nor less than an outrage on human nature productive in all probability of no beneficial results whatever. As a phase of immature development it is entitled to about the same scientific respect as the contemporaneous purging, bolusing and bloodletting medical treatment; the first blighted then and the last killed; just as both, if in use, would blight and kill now.

It would have been inconsistent with any accepted theory of human nature that the moral conditions, continually and systematically developed by the treatment which has been described, should not periodically have broken out in phases of acute mania. We can view the thing from a cold pathological and scientific point of view, observing cause and effect; at the time it was taken theologically, and a fit of madness was regarded as a manifestation of the immediate presence of the Deity. At first the acute attacks of the mania took the forms of ordinary religious persecutions, finding vent against Baptists and Quakers; then it assumed a much more interesting phase in the Salem Witchcraft craze of 1691–92. The New England historians have usually regarded this curious and interesting episode as an isolated phenomenon, to be described as such, and then palliated it by references to the far more ferocious and unthinking maniacal outbreaks of like nature in other lands at about the same time.[16] This is simply to ignore its significance. Lecky, in his *History of Rationalism*, sets forth the law as follows: "It may be stated, I believe

[15] Edwards's *Works* (ed. 1855), vol. iii, pp. 265–9; *Magnalia*, VI, chap. vii, Appendix, Ex. iv.

[16] Palfrey, vol. iv, p. 122; Ellis, *Puritan Age*, pp. 558, 559.

as an invariable truth, that, whenever a religion which rests in a great measure on a system of terrorism, and which paints in dark and forcible colors the misery of men and the power of evil spirits, is intensely realized, it will engender the belief in witchcraft or magic. The panic which its teachings will create, will overbalance the faculties of multitudes."[17] And, again, referring to the fact that during the period of the Commonwealth probably more alleged witches perished in England than in the whole period before and after, the same investigator declares that this "was simply the natural result of Puritanical teaching acting on the mind, predisposing men to see Satanic influence in life, and consequently eliciting the phenomena of witchcraft."[18] The mania of 1691–92 in Massachusetts was no isolated or inexplicable manifestation; on the contrary, it was a most noticeable instance of the operation of law: given John Winthrop's journal in 1630–40, Salem witchcraft at a somewhat later period might with safety be predicted. The community was predisposed to the epidemic; . . . Leaving this part of the story, a sterile waste, it is necessary to turn and study the concurrent course of that political activity, which in Massachusetts had from the very beginning flowed as a stream of living water beneath the thick ice-crust of theology.

I have referred to the curious but intimate sympathy in regard to all political issues which, in Massachusetts as in Scotland, existed between the people and the clergy throughout the seventeenth and eighteenth centuries. As a rule, and from the earliest times, the church and the priesthood have been a part of the governmental machinery and in closest relations with the civil authority. That it was altogether otherwise in Scotland during those two centuries Buckle attributes to the fact that for a hundred and twenty years after the establishment of Protestantism the feudal rulers of Scotland either neglected the church or persecuted it, thereby driving the clergy into the arms of the people. Hence an alliance between the two parties; and hence too the steady development of that democratic spirit which the clergy encouraged.[19] An exactly similar alliance may be studied in the evolutionary processes of Massachusetts.[20] From the beginning the ministers preached rigid conformity in religion, and stubborn independence in politics. For instance, the very ministers who met in Cambridge in September, 1637, to crush out once for all religious freedom in Massachusetts, those same ministers only twenty months before had been summoned to Boston to confer with the magistrates as to the course to be pursued if King Charles and Archbishop Laud should indeed, as was threatened, commission and send out to New England a Governor-General. When this question was referred by the magistrates to the ministers the answer came back, quick and decisive, "We ought not to accept him, but defend our lawful possessions, if we are able!" In that answer there was no superstition about the divine right of kings and obedience to rulers; no obligation to conformity: and it was prophetic. It struck the key-note which

17 *Rationalism in Europe*, vol. i, p. 37.
18 *Ibid.*, pp. 102, 125, 143, 144.

19 *History*, vol. iii, p. 191.

20 "An established priesthood is naturally the firmest support of despotism; but the course of events made that of Massachusetts revolutionary. . . . Massachusetts became the hotbed of rebellion because of this unwonted alliance between liberality and sacerdotalism." — Brooks Adams, *Emancipation of Massachusetts*, pp. 342, 362.

rang true and strong from that January, 1635, to April, 1775.

Of the course of political events in Massachusetts through its theological period and down to the year 1760, when at last political predominated over religious life, it is not necessary here to speak in detail; nor, indeed, is the story an interesting one. It can be read in its dreary details in the pages of the historians: but, after all, perhaps Hawthorne in his *True Stories,* his *Scarlet Letter,* and his *Twice Told Tales* has best embalmed most of its facts with all of its romance. It was a monotonous period of slow, provincial growth, in the course of which the community passed through a series of Indian and then of other wars, Queen Anne's war, the old French war, King George's war, holding innumerable town meetings, governing themselves absolutely in local affairs and practically in colonial, and everlastingly bickering over salaries and tenure of office with the governors appointed by the crown to rule over them. The erection of a fort at Pemaquid continually emerges; while the unfortunate provincials seem never to weary of experimenting upon themselves with every conceivable form of currency nostrum. A record less inviting to the general reader could not be found; and yet with the slow narrative of its details Palfrey fills two cumbrous volumes, nor even then does he complete it. But it was the long period of slow preparation; . . .

Massachusetts illustrated forcibly the truth of one Scripture aphorism when the fathers sinned in 1637 and the sins of the fathers were visited on the children through three and four generations until 1760. And now in closing I can only repeat what I have elsewhere said:

That in time the intellect of Massachusetts — schooled by self-government through a long struggle with nature and against foreign encroachments — did work itself out from under the incubus of superstition, prejudice and narrow conformity imposed upon it by the first generation of magistrates and ministers, cannot be denied; but it is certainly going far to infer therefrom that, in this especial case, superstition, prejudice and narrow conformity were helps instead of obstacles. It is not easy, indeed, to see how the *post ergo propter* fallacy could be carried further. It is much like arguing, because a child of robust frame and active mind survives stripes and starvation in infancy, and bad instruction and worse discipline in youth, struggling through to better things in manhood, that therefore the stripes and starvation, and bad instruction and worse discipline, in his case at least, worked well and were the cause of his subsequent excellence. It is barely possible that New England, contrary to all principle and precedent, may have profited by the harshness and bigotry which for a time suppressed all freedom of thought in Massachusetts; but it is far more likely that the slow results afterwards there achieved came notwithstanding that drawback, rather than in consequence of the discipline it afforded. Certainly the historians who with such confidence set aside all the lessons of human experience — in order to assert that, in the case of their ancestors, whatever was, was right, as well as best — would be slow to apply the same rules or draw similar conclusions in the case of such as persecuted, banished or suppressed those who thought like their ancestors.

Samuel Eliot Morison:

BUILDERS OF THE BAY COLONY

THE time has come, the Walrus said, to talk of puritanism and the puritans. I had hoped to get through this book without that disagreeable task of definition; but it cannot be done. What then is meant by puritanism, and who were the puritans?

Puritanism was a way of life based on the belief that the Bible was the word of God, and the whole word of God. Puritans were the Englishmen who endeavored to live according to that light. Having been so round, I must shade off, for puritanism has had various meanings at different times. Originally a nickname (οἱ καθαροί, *puritani*) flung about on the theological controversies of the late Roman Empire, it was revived in Queen Elizabeth's reign to describe that party of English Protestants who wished to carry out the Reformation to its logical conclusion, and purge the Anglican Church of forms and ceremonies for which there was no warrant in the Bible; or, to use a phrase of Cartwright which became a watchword for one party and a jest for their opponents, to restore the Christian Church 'pure and unspotted.' At first it was applied only to persons within the Church of England; but by 1630, the term puritan had been stretched to include separatists like the Pilgrims who obtained purity outside the Anglican communion, and even the Scots Presbyterians, who had a different organization. Further, the Church of England puritans were divided into non-conformists, who disobeyed the law rather than compromise with conscience, and the conformable puritans like John White and John Winthrop who performed or attended the prescribed services according to the Book of Common Prayer, while hoping for better things.

Beside this purely religious meaning of puritanism, there was a moral aspect. Persons who read the Bible and sincerely believed in it, adopted or attempted a very exacting code of morals; and as they believed that this code was gospel ordinance, they endeavored to enforce it on others. Such persons were originally called precisians, and were not necessarily puritans in a religious sense. The most thoroughly puritanic diary I have ever read, full of moans and groans over the mildest peccadilloes of himself and others, is that of Samuel Ward, master of Sidney Sussex College, a stout Royalist and Anglican who was expelled by Cromwell. We mean this moral preciseness when we use the term puritanism to-day; yet moral puritanism is by no means confined to the Protestant or English-speaking churches. The Catholic counter-reformation of the sixteenth century was quite as puritanic in a moral sense as the Protestant reformation. Jansenism was a puritanical movement within the Gallican Church in France; and no sect within the last century has been more puritanical in a moral sense than the Catholic

From *Builders of the Bay Colony* by Samuel Eliot Morison. Houghton Mifflin Company, 1930. Reprinted by permission.

Church in Ireland. In England there was what we might call high church puritanism, of which the 'divine Herbert' was the highest example. King Charles and Bishop Laud were both persons of high moral standards. Laud's ecclesiastical courts were as zealous to punish immorality as to enforce conformity; and the reforms that he began in the University of Oxford were continued by its later puritan rulers. If Bishop and King had not attempted religious innovations in the direction of Rome, if they had respected the ritual and doctrine of the Church as Elizabeth or even Archbishop Bancroft had left them, the puritans might never have become associated with radicalism and democracy.

And what of the political side of puritanism? Charles Borgeaud, and other political scientists, have traced democracy to puritanism. I do not think that this theory will hold water, although there is something in it. The Englishman of 1630 was politically mature, compared with other Europeans. He was beginning to feel his way toward popular government, and during the Interregnum he went far on that road. As we have seen in the case of the Salem Church, the congregational polity which one branch of the puritans favored, made laymen the governing body of the church. But the connection between puritanism and political liberalism was fortuitous. English puritans in 1630 rallied to representative government and traditional English liberty because that was their only refuge against innovating Bishops and a high church King; but in New England where they had things their own way, their political spirit was conservative and their temper autocratic. If American democracy came out of puritan New England (and it may equally well be traced to

Virginia), it came from the English and not the puritan in our ancestors, and from the newness not the puritanism of New England.

We would do well then to remember that puritanism in the seventeenth century had a purely religious connotation. I will not detain my readers here with a summary of their beliefs and practices; these will appear as the lives of those commonwealth builders, puritans all, unfold. Yet pardon me if I caution you against certain current delusions about the early puritans upon which historians have placed the stamp of authority. The one is that they were mainly preoccupied with hell and damnation. On the contrary, fire-and-brimstone sermons, and poems such as Wigglesworth's 'Day of Doom,' belong to a later generation or to the eighteenth century, when puritan pastors tried to frighten their backsliding congregations into good behavior. The second delusion is that puritanism is synonymous with Calvinism. Broadly speaking the English puritan theologians were Calvinist in their theology rather than Lutheran or Arminian; but being learned in their ancient tongues they derived their ideas mainly from the Bible and the Fathers. Calvin's 'Institutes' was never to them a sacred book, and I have found Calvin less frequently quoted in their writings than English theologians like Ames, Perkins, and Whitaker. A third delusion is that puritans were prohibitionists, or indirectly responsible for prohibition. Their faith put more stress on the joys of the inner life than on those of the senses, but they made no attempt to proscribe one of God's good creatures, whose temperate use was sanctioned by the Bible, and by our Lord's example. Finally, readers of New England history must be cautioned against ascribing to puritanism alone a coarseness that was common to the age, and a bigotry that was common to all Christian sects, and still is far too common. We will not often find breadth of mind among the English puritans; but we will find a spiritual depth that belongs only to the great ages of religious experience.

John Winthrop was happy to have lived in the golden age of English puritanism, when some of its early fanaticism had been sloughed off, without losing the bloom of youth. It had not altogether broken with the stately and cadenced ritual of the Book of Common Prayer; it had grasped firm hold of the evangelistic principle, the 'tidings of great joy' that our Saviour brought to men. Whatever puritanism may have come to mean in later ages — and I will freely admit that its more recent manifestations have been negative, narrow, and altogether unlovely — it meant three hundred years ago, a high sincerity of purpose, an integrity of life, and an eager searching for the voice of God. The intellectual strength of the puritan was his knowledge of the Bible; the moral strength of the puritan was his direct approach to God. No puritan ever said, as did the children of Israel when they heard the thunder and the trumpet blasts on Mount Sinai, 'Let not God speak to us, lest we die.' His home, his study, his meeting-house, were filled with the reverberations of the awful and gracious voice for which he listened. If he rejected the intercession of the saints, it was because he would meet God face to face. If he despised the ancient pageantry of worship, it was because he would have no false and sensual symbols between him and his Redeemer. Often, like the ancient Hebrews, he misunderstood the voice of God. Often he mistook for it the echo of his own wants and passions. But the desire to hear it, the

sense that life consisted in hearing and obeying it, never left him.

* * *

Although religion was the dynamic force which gave the Bay colony character and consistency, it was not an all-absorbing interest. Even puritans did not live by faith alone, nor did puritanism blight the creative and expansive side of human nature. Man's urge to build and create, his age-long yearning for comfort and security, his sense of form and beauty, found outlet in early New England, as in few other settlements of like age. He who best combined these aspects of life with the religious was John Hull, captain of militia and owner of ships; business man and magistrate, master of the mint, and deacon of the church, first in a long line of master goldsmiths who enriched the churches and homes of New England with beautiful examples of their art.

The men and women whose acquaintance we are making, moved in a colorful scene, 'incomparably more picturesque than at present,' as Hawthorne wrote. Yet Hawthorne, more than any man, was responsible for the somber picture of early New England dear to popular illustrators, and already embalmed in tradition. A brooding sense of gloom; a village of log houses, pierced only by a few square-paned windows; a stalwart puritan dressed in black except for a broad white collar; on his arm a woman in mouse-colored gray, wearing a white coif. As a matter of fact, the puritans normally dressed in bright colors, they never built a log house, and the moral and Sabbatarian atmosphere, which doubtless would prove depressing to us, was what they came to America to enjoy.

Log cabins were introduced to America by the Swedes and Finns on the Delaware, and did not appear on the New England frontier until the eighteenth century. The first temporary shelters in Massachusetts were conical huts of branches and turf, such as the charcoal-burners used in England, or wattle-and-daub cottages with thatched roofs. These were soon replaced by houses of hewn and sawn timber. A frame of stout oak (post and sill, plate and beam, neatly mortised and fastened with wooden trunnels) was erected around a central chimney of brick,[1] a filling of clay, straw, and rubble placed between the joists, the outside sheathed with riven clapboard, and the inside plastered or sheathed with wide upright pine boards. Window-openings were sometimes single and sometimes grouped, but always hung with leaded casements and glazed with diamond panes. Roofs were steep-pitched as if for thatch, which the first-comers used, and were slow to abandon for cedar shingles. Salem and Boston in John Hull's day resembled more a town of mediæval Europé, than anything that exists in America to-day. It is not until 1680 that we find a building in Massachusetts (the Province House) which owed anything to Palladio or Inigo Jones. The puritan housewright followed the mediæval tradition, and his detail was gothic. His frame was planned for use, and his house was built to the frame, instead of with a view to effect and proportion, as in the architecture of the Renaissance. Similarly the cabinet makers, iron-workers and silversmiths brought over the best traditions of mediæval craftsmanship. Their art was dynamic, not academic.

Far from condemning the beautiful, the generation which planned the New England villages, divided the fields, and built the first houses, seemed incapable of making anything ugly. If their laying out of homestead, village common, stone wall, road, and meeting-house was unconscious, the more to the credit of their instinct; for it was done in harmony with the lay of the land, the contours of valley and slope, the curve of stream and shore. Cambridge, on a level plain like a bowling green, was laid out square; across the river the paths and lanes of Boston followed a scalloped sea-front and looped around three mamelons. At first the New England village was crude and raw with mud and stump-studded fields. Given time for flowers to bloom in dooryards and wine-glass elms to rise about the comely houses, it grew into the sort of unconscious beauty that comes of ordered simplicity. . . .

The Massachusetts puritans disliked extravagance; but they appreciated comeliness, whether in a ship, a house, or a woman; and they loved bright-colored paint on ships and houses — but not on women. An example in point is Captain John Endecott, so rigid an iconoclast that he defaced the cross on the English ensign as an emblem of idolatry and superstition. Yet Captain Endecott tricked out the trim of his great house at Salem with scarlet paint, hung carved bargeboards under the eaves, and lived there well and generously. Puritan costume was distinguished from court costume by comparative plainness, and absence of lace and spangle, rather than by color. Only the ministers followed the ancient sacerdotal tradition in wearing black. 'Sad colored' clothes there were, of russett, gray, green and dark blue, and for working clothes men wore leather and undyed homespun woolens; but on great occasions your puritan might be gaudy. Governor Bradford left a red waistcoat with silver buttons, a

[1] Originally the chimneys, even of such important people as the Downings, were 'catted'; i.e., built of wood and daubed with clay.

colored hat, a violet cloak, and a Turkey-red grogram suit. Governor Bellingham wears a scarlet cloak in his portrait, painted in 1641. A snatch of inventories in the Essex County probate records, for 1636–44, yields a purple cloth suit, doublet, and hose; a green doublet, a long blue coat with silver buttons; blue, black, red, and green waistcoats; purple and russett gowns; aprons of green and tawny; blue and red petticoats; plain and embroidered women's caps of various bright colors. As for headwear, the puritan did wear on occasion the broad-brimmed, high-crowned, black felt hat dear to modern illustrators, but not exclusively. Each servant of the Massachusetts Bay Company in 1629 was provided with one, doubtless for Sabbath wear; but he also drew a Monmouth cap (a sort of close-fitting cloth beret), and five red knitted caps. 'Portugal caps' are mentioned in John Hull's orders; skull caps were worn in the house by ministers and magistrats. Thirty years later, John Hull is importing from England hats of various shapes and colors, blue duffels and red penistones, red and yellow flannels, red galant cloth and blue ditto: red and blue worsted stockings. 'Sad colours' are wanted only in the kersies and serges; black taffetas he found impossible to sell.

As to interior decorations and furnishings; here is an inventory to make the collector envious, from the household of the first President of Harvard College. In a lawsuit over the estate, an ancient domestic thus testified about the contents of the President's house:

Eleven feather beds or Downs, all well furnished. one had phlox and cherry curtains ingrain with a Deep silk Fringe on the Vallance and a smaller on the Curtain, and a coverlet made of Red Kersey and barred with green lace round the sides and two down the middle. Also there apertained to that bed an outlining the quilt, also another a blew serge suit,[2] very rich and costly curtains and valances laced and fringed, and a blew rug to the bed. Also a Greene suit in the same manner, also another Red wrought suite with a stoole and all things complete. Also a Canopy bed with curtains, a chest of Drawers, of which one of that chest was full with linnen, a Damask Suite, several Diaper Suites, a fine yellow Rug, with a starr and with abundance of Flaxen Linnen for common use. In another part of the Chest of Drawers tapes and tafetys for screen and shades. A paire of Greate brasse andirons, A paire of smaller brasse andirons, Brasse candle-sticks of sorts, A greate brasse pot, Brasse of all sorts useful for a family, Pewter of several sorts. Plate of all sorts great and small, 29 Spoons, A very fair salt with 3 knobs on top of it,[3] 3 silver pitchers of lesser sort, A great silver tankard, 4 mugs to stand on a table, quite fine; 6 porringers. 1 small, 3 great bowles; 4 mugs and a pot, Silver grater with cover. 6 plain trenchers, Plate. Also Blanketts, Coverletts and Rugs.

This was the inventory of a well-to-do family. The poorer sort lived in two-room cottages often with a thatched roof and an outside oven, and no cellar; but so far as we can learn from the inventories they never put up long with an earth floor, which satisfies even the better peasants in Brittany. For £21 in 1640 a Boston weaver builds a house 14 by 16 feet, framed, sheathed and finished, with a 'chamber floare' and a 'cellar floare.' They slept under coarse woolen rugs on flock-beds, and the furniture was made by the goodman with his axe and lathe. An iron kettle or two, a skillet, a frying pan and

[2] Used in the old sense of 'set.'

[3] This is the 'great salt' which was given to Harvard College by one of Mrs. Dunster's sons. One of the same model is shown in the illustrations of Edward Winslow's silver. It will be noted that there are no forks in the inventory. Governor Winthrop brought over one in a case, doubtless regarded as a great curiosity.

wooden spoons and trenchers made up ✓ the kitchen equipment. It is striking evidence of the standards which even the common people had reached, that we seldom hear of women working in the fields, although they took full charge of the dairy. Perhaps puritan standards of housewifery were too exacting to permit of field labor, and the household spinning and weaving consumed all the 'precious time' not devoted to preparing food and drink. Nor is there evidence that the poorer people housed animals under the same roof with themselves, as the peasants in parts of Europe do to this day. . . .

In the art of painting, there is nothing to boast about. The earliest portrait painting in the colonies was done by limners, who painted taverns and shop signs, coats of arms for hatchments, or for the panels of carriages. A Boston limner once offered to paint the portrait of the venerable Master John Wilson, but met with a flat refusal; for some of the stricter puritans regarded portraits as vanities. Although there have survived twelve or fourteen Boston portraits of the period 1666–1686, very few can be assigned to a definite artist. Evert Duyckinck, a Dutch limner of New York, is known to have painted the excellent 'Athenæum' portrait of Chief-Justice Stoughton at Dorchester in 1685; but it is only a guess to assign the portrait of Governor Bellingham painted in 1641 and signed 'W. R.' to a local map-maker named William Read. There are in existence several alleged portraits of New England worthies with inscriptions assigning them to Bostonians, and some authorities on colonial portraiture accept these as genuine. When one reflects that it takes only a neat inscription to lift an anonymous portrait out of a London junk-shop to an 'early American' worth something in four

figures, one will be cautious in accepting such 'discoveries' unless they have a well-attested pedigree. There is not known to be in existence a single landscape or genre painting or even drawing of a New England subject until well on in the eighteenth century.

Here is no stick to beat the puritans, however. Pioneering is not conducive to artistry. The age of colonization was the greatest age of Spanish art; yet the two Americas provided hardly a subject for a Spanish brush; and of the thousands of Dutch interiors of the seventeenth century, not one is of New Netherland. Even Magna Graecia could show little achievement in the arts to compare with Athens; and in modern times, whether in New Spain, New France, or the overseas dependencies of England, at least a century and a half had to elapse before the colony could produce anything in creative art comparable with that of the mother country.

The only medium for sculpture in New England was the gravestone; and it was improved to the full. The first generation was content with a simple inscription and a crude death's head; the second and third generations showed excellent taste in conventional borders of foliage and fruit, in the lettering, and in the composition of the hour-glass, scythe, skull, angel's wings, and other emblems of mortality and resurrection. In the examples here reproduced we find the beginning of a true folk art, which followed a consistent development through the next century as the puritan creed softened, replacing the skull and crossbones by a winged cherub, and finally attempting a portrait. Few names of gravestone-cutters of the seventeenth century have been preserved, but the nature of the stones proves that the work must have been done locally.

What, then, becomes of the favorite notion of 'stark' puritanism, with its cult of ugliness, and inveterate hostility to the arts? Only this: that puritanism was not a way of life favorable to the development of the highest art, since it forbade the use of symbolism in religion (with the fortunate exception of the Lord's Supper) and discouraged extravagance and display. By rejecting religious music, religious sculpture, and religious painting, as misleading symbols diverting man from direct communion with God, the puritan deliberately closed some of the principal outlets for the æsthetic sense. Yet the men of the Bay Colony, magistrates and ministers, deacons and church members, have left sufficient evidence that they appreciated beauty in the things of daily use, and were capable of producing it themselves. The evidence is so concrete and conclusive as to preclude chance; nor is it chance that so many of the best architects, sculptors, painters, musicians, poets, and prose writers of America, have been descendants of Bay Colony puritans. The puritans of that day had no grudge against civilization, only against its corruptions; and he who dedicates his life to the beauty of holiness, is not far from the sight of all beauty.

Samuel Eliot Morison: THE PURITAN PRONAOS

Scientific Strivings

IT appears to be a common notion that the New England puritans were hostile or indifferent to science, while nourishing and coddling various pseudo-scientific superstitions, such as astrology, demonology, and witchcraft. The German social historian Troeltsch declared that puritanism was hostile to natural science, wishing all things to be explained supernaturally — the same old charge that has been made time and again against Catholicism.[1] Dr. Dorothy Simpson, on the contrary, finds that the principal English scientists of the 'century of genius,' those who founded the Royal Society, observed nature, and made experiments, were men of puritan background.[2]

In the colonies we find the relation between puritanism and science to be much the same as between puritanism and literature. Religion proved a stimulus rather than a restraint, because the clerical leaders of the community were educated men, curious about what was going on, eager to keep in touch with the movements of their day, and receptive to new scientific theories. The scientific production of colonial New England was negligible compared even with that of Mexico; yet more than in other English colonies. As a rough test, let us see how many colonists were elected fellows by

[1] Quoted in H. J. C. Grierson, *Cross Currents in English Literature of the Seventeenth Century* (London, 1929), p. 192 n.

[2] Paper read before the History of Science Society at Washington in December, 1934, and which Dean Simpson kindly communicated to me.

From *The Puritan Pronaos* by Samuel Eliot Morison. New York University Press, 1936. Reprinted by permission.

the Royal Society of London, the great scientific academy of the English-speaking world: one from the Carolinas, three from Virginia, three from Pennsylvania (including Benjamin Franklin), and eleven from New England. And one of the New Englanders, Governor John Winthrop of Connecticut, was proposed for membership before the Royal Society obtained its charter, and chosen fellow at the first regular election, May 20, 1663.

The scientific strivings of New England are, moreover, a test of their receptivity to new ideas. For the puritan colonies were founded, and their college of liberal arts established, before the New Philosophy (as the new science was generally called) had obtained a foothold in the English universities. . . .

Astronomy affords the best test of the New England attitude toward science, for the astronomical theories and discoveries of Copernicus, Galileo, and Kepler were not only the most spectacular, but the most disturbing of the age. Copernicus's hypothesis that the earth spun around on its own axis and revolved about the sun; Galileo's demonstration that God was not the immediate source of astral energy; Kepler's proof that the planets followed, not the circular path which was supposed to reflect divine perfection, but elliptical orbits, moved man first to astonishment, then to pain, and then to anger. It mattered not whether he was Catholic or Protestant, since the reformers had accepted the same philosophical explanation of reality as the schoolmen; doubtless the great majority of Protestants approved when in 1633 the Inquisition forced Galileo to recant his heliocentric theory, as 'contrary to Holy Scripture.' Oxford, though she had a chair of astronomy as early as 1619, wanted an exponent of the new astronomy for thirty years more. When Maest-

lin, the German astronomer who encouraged Galileo and taught Kepler, wrote a college textbook of astronomy, he dared not, because of his official position in the University of Heidelberg, adopt the Copernican hypothesis, but declared that the earth was immobile. Astronomy was the dangerous subject in the universities around 1620, as economics and philosophy in our own day; the thing for which professors got fired because they did not 'coöperate.' Catholic universities were even forbidden to teach Copernican astronomy until the end of the eighteenth century; of course many if not most of them disregarded the prohibition.

Hence, we need not be surprised that the first generation of college students in New England were taught the astronomy of the ancients, the Ptolemaic system. . . .

Not long were our colonial students allowed to retain their cosmographic innocence; and as soon as they learned about the New Astronomy, they were eager to tell the world about it. *Astronomia Instaurata* by Vincent Wing, the first Englishman who made a satisfactory popular exposition of the Copernican system, was apparently 'adopted' at Harvard shortly after its first appearance in 1656; for an essay based on it is printed in the annual New England almanac for 1659. These almanacs, as we have seen, were compiled by Harvard tutors or graduate students, and often employed by them as a medium for college poetry. Zechariah Brigden, who had worked his way through college by 'ringinge the bell and waytinge in the hall,' received the almanac assignment for 1659, and started a new fashion by using his empty space for a popular essay on astronomy. . . .[3]

The reception of this almanac is significant. Both President Chauncy and John

[3] Reprinted in *The New England Quarterly*, VII, 9–12.

Winthrop, Jr., sent copies of it to the Reverend John Davenport, the famous minister of New Haven. Mr. Davenport observed that Galileo, Gassendi, and Kepler meant nothing to him; that the young author appeared to be setting himself up as the eighth sage; that we lived in a fixed place, not a revolving planet, and that the objections from Scripture were not answered. 'However it be,' he writes to John Winthrop, Jr., 'let him injoy his opinion; and I shall rest in what I have learned, til more cogant arguments be produced.'

I wish to rub this in! Much has been written about the bigotry of the New England clergy, and Davenport was one of the least liberal of that group; yet he does not demand that Brigden be fired from Harvard, or kept out of the pulpit. He simply agrees to disagree with the young radical. The new astronomy, which had to fight the church and the clergy in almost every other country, was accepted by and even propagated by the clergy in New England. The clerical government of the college sponsored these annual almanacs which, almost every year from 1659 on, contained a popular essay on the new astronomy; and clergymen like the Mathers were the chief patrons and promoters of the new science.

The pseudo-science of astrology seems never to have had any standing at Harvard. A long series of commencement theses, beginning in 1653, prove that it was the favorite butt of undergraduate disputants at these academic festivities.

Fortunately for the new astronomy, the seventeenth century was rich in comets, the observation of which added greatly to our knowledge of the universe, and enabled Newton to correlate Kepler's discoveries with his own, and work out the laws of gravitation. Theologians had long considered comets within their province, as heavenly portents of disaster; and it was not without a struggle that they relinquished these 'blazing stars' to the scientists. The first comet to stimulate literary activity in New England was that which appeared at the turn of the years 1664–1665. Samuel Danforth, the almanac poet, was now minister of Roxbury, but retained his interest in astronomy. In 1665 he had printed at Cambridge a tract of one hundred and twenty-two pages called "An Astronomic Description of the late Comet or Blazing Star, with a brief Theological Application thereof." And for the Almanac of 1665 Alexander Nowell, who had graduated the previous June, wrote an essay called "The Suns Prerogative Vindicated," quoting observations by European astronomers (such as Seth Ward, the Savilian Professor at Oxford) through 'optick tubes' (telescopes), and concluding with remarks on comets. Both the young man and the older minister admit that comets proceed from natural causes, are subject to mathematical laws, and are composed of the same stuff as the stars — a somewhat advanced position in 1665; but they insist nevertheless that comets are divine portents of disasters. For surely God is a better mathematician than we![4]

Before the next important comet came along, Harvard College had acquired a telescope from John Winthrop, Jr., then Governor of Connecticut. The younger Winthrop was easily first in scientific interest among New Englanders in the seventeenth century. Educated largely through his own readings and extensive

[4] Nowell's essay was thought so good by John Josselyn, the English traveler, that he printed it in his *Two Voyages to New England* (London, 1674). It is reprinted in Sibley, *Harvard Graduates*, II, 149–151. Considerable correspondence between Increase Mather and English divines on comets will be found in *Collections of the Massachusetts Historical Society*, VIII.

travels (since he had spent but two years at Trinity College, Dublin), he came to New England at the age of twenty-five, bringing with him a large library full of scientific books of which the surviving remnant, in the Society Library of New York, contains fifty-two relating to chemistry and alchemy, thirty-three on medicine, twenty-seven on mathematics and physics, twelve on witchcraft, astrology, and occult lore.[5] Winthrop, like many intellectuals of his day, was interested in almost every branch of science. He was a practising physician, and dispensed medicines of his own compounding to the poor. He prospected for minerals, assayed ores that he found in New England, dabbled in alchemy, organized the first ironworks and salt-pans in New England, and showed a keen interest in optics and astronomy. But his principal interest, as his books indicate, was in chemistry, which had not yet attained the dignity of a separate discipline, but was regarded as a branch of physics, somewhat under ill repute with the *cognoscenti* because the object of most of the early chemists was to discover the philosopher's stone and transmute base metals into gold. Winthrop's collection of works on chemistry and alchemy includes several books that belonged to John Dee, the celebrated mathematician, astrologer, and reputed magician of Queen Elizabeth's reign.

There were not many people in New England who could share Winthrop's chemical tastes and enthusiasm. One of them, George Stirk or Starkey, a lad from Bermuda, graduated from the college in 1646 and shortly after returned to England, where he became a famous practitioner of medicine and experimental alchemist. Robert Child (M.D. Padua),

another of Winthrop's scientific friends, was expelled from Massachusetts in 1647 for daring to ask toleration for Presbyterians. But Jonathan Brewster and Gershom Bulkeley remained. The former, son of Elder Brewster of the Pilgrim church, maintained a trading post at the site of Norwich, Connecticut, when Winthrop was living at New London, and like him had a private laboratory for chemical experiments. Bulkeley did the same at his parsonage on the Connecticut River. These three were constantly interchanging books. Among Winthrop's English scientific friends and correspondents were Robert Boyle, the Earl of Clarendon, Sir Kenelm Digby, Prince Rupert, Sir Christopher Wren, and Samuel Hartlib; among his European correspondents were Glauber, Kepler, and Van Helmont. He became, as we have seen, one of the earliest fellows of the Royal Society. Sir Kenelm Digby and others begged him to live in London, and not to hide his light in a remote corner of the world; but he remained faithful to New England, and died while leading Connecticut safely through the dangers of King Philip's War.

One of Winthrop's many scientific interests was astronomy. His library contained the second edition of Tycho Brahe's *Astronomia Instaurata*, Kepler *de Stella Nova*, and two other works by him. On Winthrop's return from England in 1663, he brought a three-and-a-half-foot telescope, the first that is known to have been imported into the English colonies. . . . In 1672 he presented the college with his telescope and sundry attachments, which were enthusiastically acknowledged by the three tutors, one of them, Alexander Nowell, who had already written on comets.[6] Shortly after

---

[5] The library is described by Dr. C. A. Browne, in *Isis*, XI (1928), 328–341.

[6] *N.E.Q.*, VII, 17–18.

the Governor wrote to his son in Boston to inquire if the college students had observed anything worth while; but his reply is lost, and we know nothing of what use was made of the college telescope for eight years.

In the year 1680 there appeared in the eastern sky a great comet, sometime called Newton's Comet, which excited astronomers all the way from Poland to Mexico, terrified the ignorant, provoked sundry controversies between scientists and theologians,[7] and impelled Isaac Newton along the line of reasoning that led to his greatest discovery. Thomas Brattle, the young Harvard graduate who later complained of the slight assistance he had in mathematical studies, observed the comet of 1680 through the college telescope, printed his observations in the local almanac for 1681, and communicated them to Flamsteed, the Royal Astronomer at Greenwich, who in turn sent them to his friend Newton. In the *Principia*, after quoting several 'rude' observations of this comet, Newton says that 'those made by Montenari, Hooke, Ango, and the observer in New England, taking the position of the comet with reference to the fixed stars, are better.' This, Brattle wrote to Flamsteed many years later, 'was no small comfort to me, that I was none of the last of all the Lags.'

Considering his limited equipment, Brattle's observations are remarkable. Independently he recognized the fact that a comet which disappeared at perihelion into the glare of the sun's rays and reappeared on the other side of the sun was one and the same comet. His observations were valuable to Newton because, being based on fixed stars rather

than on azimuths and altitudes, they helped him to determine the orbital elements of a comet moving in an ellipse. Hence our little college telescope, used by a careful and intelligent observer, contributed its mite toward helping Newton to test Kepler's three laws, to work out the law of gravitation, and to write the great *Principia*.

The college telescope did not long remain idle. In 1682, Halley's Comet made one of its periodical visits to the earth, and was viewed through our 'optick tube' by both Mathers. Increase Mather incorporated his observations, with much reading that he had done in Hevelius's *Cometographia* (Danzig, 1668) in a work called "*Kometographia, or a Discourse Concerning Comets*" (Boston, 1683). Cotton Mather had something to say on the subject in an almanac that he compiled, the "Boston Ephemeris" for 1683. His younger brother, Nathaniel Mather, before graduating from the college in 1685, published in the "Boston Ephemeris" for that year a list of astronomical discoveries which shows that he was keeping up with the work of Hooke, Cassini, and Flamsteed, as reported in the "Philosophical Transactions" of the Royal Society. Thomas Brattle himself contributed to the "Philosophical Transactions" some observations he and Henry Newman made by a brass quadrant with telescopic sights, of an eclipse at Cambridge in 1694. By the turn of the century the college had acquired a new telescope, a foot longer than Winthrop's; and with this Brattle made observations until his death in 1713 — after which William Brattle was elected Fellow of the Royal Society on the strength of what his brother Thomas had done.

Increase Mather had preached two sermons entitled "Heaven's Alarm to the World" and "The Latter Sign" (Boston,

---

[7] One of these is well described by Irving A. Leonard, in his paper on Don Carlos de Sigüenza, the Mexican astronomer (*University of California Publications in History*, XVIII), pp. 58–61.

1682) on the occasion of the Comet of 1680. *Kometographia* was a more elaborate treatise, in one hundred and fifty or more pages. Two only of the ten chapters related to the nature of comets; the other eight, on the history of comets, were attempts to prove that their appearance always portended remarkable or calamitous events. Mather was familiar with the work of Hooke and Kepler, and the latest publications of the Royal Society; he admitted that comets proceeded from natural causes, but insisted that their appearance could not be predicted. For he had as yet no knowledge of Halley's identification of the Comet of 1683 with those that had appeared in 1531 and 1607. And although Increase still clung to the portentous aspect of comets, his point of view was worlds apart from that of the ecclesiastics who had condemned Galileo in 1633, for an hypothesis that was contrary to Holy Writ. Mather accepted what the scientists had observed; but as the facts of history seemed to prove a time-correlation between the appearance of comets and disasters in human affairs, it was still reasonable to suppose that there was some connection.[8]

Those were busy years in Increase Mather's study. In 1683 he and a number of Boston gentlemen, including Samuel Willard, formed a scientific club: the Philosophical Society they called it. This was the first child of the Royal Society of London; the Dublin Philosophical Society, founded the following year, being the second.[9] The Boston group met fortnightly for a number of years 'for conference upon improvements in philosophy and additions to the stores of natural history.'

Witchcraft[10]

It seems probable that Mather hoped that through this club there might be compiled a natural history of New England, according to the 'rules and method described by that learned and excellent person Robert Boyle, Esq.';[11] and he might even have tried it himself, had he not already begun a more congenial compilation, "An Essay for the Recording of Illustrious Providences." And with this book begins the history of the Salem witchcraft delusion, which provides a tragic anti-climax to the scientific advance that we have been chronicling so far.

The Mathers and their learned contemporaries were not only interested in witchcraft as priests, but as scientists. Witchcraft was one of the numerous classes of phenomena, such as light, heat, comets, growth of plants, and human anatomy, that men of science were investigating; only it had a more immediate and emotional appeal because of

Society, however, petered out in a few years. The latest possible reference I have seen to it in Increase Mather's diary is dated June 30, 1693.

[10] The literature of witchcraft in New England is vast. George Lyman Kittredge, *Witchcraft in Old and New England* (Harvard University Press, 1929) places the Salem outburst in its proper setting, and is completely documented, but has little detail. G. L. Burr, *Narratives of Witchcraft* (Original Narratives Series, 1914) reprints some of the essential documents and narratives, with an introduction that differs in several important points from Kittredge. For witchcraft in Boston, and the part played by the Mathers, there is no better account than that of W. F. Poole in Justin Winsor, *The Memorial History of Boston, 1630–1880* (Boston, 1880–1881), II, 131–171.

[8] 'The interesting feature' of Mather's *Kometographia*, says Preserved Smith (*History of Modern Culture*, I, 430), 'is its erudition.' And on p. 439 he shows that Mather's position was exactly that of the humane and cultivated John Evelyn.

[9] Preserved Smith, *op. cit.*, I, 171. The Boston

[11] Preface to *Illustrious Providences*, last page.

the terror that it aroused and its supposed connection with the devil, whom
it was the particular business of parsons
to fight. As George Lyman Kittredge
has shown, almost every English scientific contemporary of the Mathers who
has left his opinion on record believed
in witchcraft;[12] and if examples are
wanted of men of science taking a particular interest in demonology and witchcraft, we have not far to seek. 'It was
typical of the seventeenth century situation that . . . Henry More, the Cambridge
rationalist and neo-Platonist, after prov-
ing his faith in the language of loftiest
Metaphysics, should proceed to buttress
it by stories of "Coskinomancy" or of the
"vomiting of Cloth stuck with Pins, Nails,
and Needles." '[13] And Joseph Glanvil,
F.R.S. and skeptic, after delivering a dev-
astating blow to the Aristotelian tradition,
and eloquently defending modern philosophy and the experimental method in his
"Vanity of Dogmatizing," proceeded to
open a Pandora-box of witchcraft and
apparitions in his *Sadducismus Trium-
phatus* (1681).[14] The recording or remarkable providences had been, as we
have seen, a leading motive of the early
New England chroniclers, and of historians like Morton and Hubbard. Acting
on a suggestion of Matthew Poole, an
English divine for whom the New Englanders had great respect, a meeting of
ministers of the Massachusetts Colony
issued and circulated in 1681 "Some Proposals concerning the Recording of Illus-

trious Providences," the results of which
Increase Mather was asked to collect and
work up in a book.[15]

The result, which was very different
from the Natural History of New England suggested by Robert Boyle, was
published as "An Essay for the Recording of Illustrious Providences" at Boston
in 1684. Three of the twelve chapters
concerned 'Things Preternatural which
have hapned in New England,' mostly
witchcrafts; and other tales of demons,
wizards, and witches; the rest of the book
was devoted to shipwrecks, thunder-
storms, tempests, remarkable escapes in
the Indian wars, stories of people being
struck blind and dumb, 'the woful end
of drunkards,' and the like. Much the
same material is to be found in the early
"Philosophical Transactions" of the Royal
Society, in the *Ephemerides Medico-
Physicae*, a German scientific annual, and
in Renaudot's *Conférences du Bureau
d'Adresse*, from which Mather frequently quotes. Mather had read and
considered the arguments of anti-witch-
craft writers, like Scot, Ady, and Webster; but, as Mr. Kittredge has shown,
these early skeptics admitted so much in
the way of demons and spooks that their
position was far less logical than that of
scientists like Glanvil who went the
whole way with the witch-hunters.

In 1688 there occurred a witchcraft
case in Boston. Four children of one of
the Mathers' parishioners went into fits
and accused an old woman with whom
they had had an altercation about the
family wash, of having bewitched them.
The poor creature confessed she had
made a compact with the devil, and was
discovered to have the traditional witch
apparatus of rag dolls representing the
victims which she stroked or pinched to

---

[12] G. L. Kittredge, *Witchcraft in Old and New
England.*

[13] Basil Willey, *The Seventeenth Century Background* (London, 1934), p. 168.

[14] An excellent discussion of Glanvil, whose *Sadducismus* and earlier editions under other titles
were well known to the Mathers, and frequently
quoted in their works, is in Basil Willey, *op. cit.*,
chapter ix.

[15] Printed in preface to Increase Mather, *Illustrious Providences* (1684).

torment them.[16] The woman was tried and found guilty, and executed for witchcraft, but the children's convulsions, ranting, and riding invisible horses, continued. Cotton Mather took the oldest girl, aged thirteen, into his family, soothed her and prayed with her as a Christian psychiatrist might do in a similar case of nerves today, kept secret the names of the persons she accused, and cured her, completely. If the girls who started the trouble at Salem had been similarly dealt with, that frenzy would not have gone so far as it did.[17] Unfortunately Mather's vanity at this favorable outcome of his efforts was such that he rushed into print with his "Memorable Providences" (Boston, 1689) describing the Goodwin case, with all its symptoms in detail; and just as newspaper stories of crime seem to stimulate more people to become criminals, so "Memorable Providences" may well have had a pernicious power of suggestion in that troubled era. That it had any such purpose cannot honestly be maintained by anyone who takes the trouble to read the book; but it is always convenient to have a scapegoat to take the guilt of a community after it has gone mad. Robert Calef, who had it in for Cotton Mather, tied a tin can to him after the frenzy was over; and it has rattled and banged through the pages of superficial and popular historians. Even today the generally accepted version of the Salem tragedy is that Cotton Mather worked it up, aided and abetted by his fellow parsons, in order to drive people back to church.

Yet the terrible outbreak at Salem Village in 1692 needed no clerical belief in witchcraft to bring it about. It arose, as witchcraft epidemics had usually arisen in Europe, during a troubled period, the *Decennium Luctuosum* of New England history when the people were uneasy with rebellions, changes of government, and Indian attacks; and in a community that had for several years been torn by factions. Salem Village, now Danvers, was an outlying parish of Salem township. It had no school, the people were poor, and their ministers had been of rather low grade. A group of girls aged from nine to nineteen began early in 1692 to simulate the physical jerks and shrieks that had been manifested by the Goodwin girls in Boston a few years before. They accused Tituba, a half-breed slave in the minister's family, and two poor old women, of having bewitched them. At this point a good spanking administered to the younger girls, and lovers provided for the older ones, might have stopped the whole thing. Instead, the slave was flogged by her master into confessing witchcraft; and to save herself accused two ancient goodwives of being her confederates. The vicious circle was started. The 'afflicted children,' finding themselves the object of unusual attention, and with the exhibitionism natural to young girls, persisted in their accusations for fear of being found out; and a state of neurosis developed similar to that of the shell-shocked soldier torn between fear of death and fear of disgrace. Those accused implicated others to escape the gallows, and confessed broomstick rides, witches' sabbaths, copulation with the devil, and anything that was expected of them. Honest folk who declared the whole thing hokum were cried

---

16 Dr. Alice Hamilton in *American Mercury*, X, 71–75, tells of the same apparatus being used by Italian witch-doctors in Chicago, in the present century.

17 Mather, to his credit, proposed to do this; but the local magistrates refused to accept his advice. Justin Winsor, ed., *The Memorial History of Boston*, II, 145–146.

out upon for witches; and in May, 1692, when Governor Sir William Phips arrived in Boston, several dozen alleged witches were in jail awaiting trial. The Governor appointed a special court composed of worthy magistrates, some of them college graduates, and presided over by William Stoughton, who had also been a fellow of New College, Oxford. This panel of learned magistrates became infected with the panic; they declined to follow the best rules for detecting witches laid down by professional English witch-hunters, and urged on them, collectively and individually, by the ministers.[18] Before they adjourned in September, 1692, nineteen persons and two dogs had been hanged for witches, and one, the brave Giles Corey, was pressed to death according to the English common law, for refusing to plead guilty or not guilty in order to save his property for his family.

In the face of this terrible frenzy, the intellectual class as a whole kept a cowardly silence. They all believed in witchcraft, to be sure; but those who had given the matter any thought knew that the rules of the game were not being observed by the court; that people were being condemned on 'spectral evidence' alone, on accusations by alleged victims, of whom the devil was supposed to have taken possession. Yet they kept silent, until twenty persons had been done to death. For, as Palfrey the historian observed, New Englanders have an 'ingrained reverence for law as such.' Hence, many who knew perfectly well that the court was condemning innocent

people held their tongues, lest they bring the judges and the government into contempt.[19] How true that analysis is, and how it recalls the actions of wise and good people in the same commonwealth, in a recent miscarriage of justice there, that I need not name! Cotton Mather wrote letters to the judges, but he did not speak loudly enough. After the Salem frenzy had subsided, he recorded in his diary:

> I was always afraid of proceeding to convict and condemn any Person, as a Confoederate with afflicting Daemons, upon so feeble an Evidence as a spectral Representation. Accordingly, I ever testified against it, both publickly and privately: and in my letters to the Judges, I particularly besought them that they would by no means admit it. . . . Nevertheless, on the other side, I saw in most of the Judges, a most charming Instance of Prudence and Patience, and I knew their exemplary Piety . . .[20]

So he could not bring himself to denounce such wise and good men publicly, as they deserved.

Such reticence or cowardice on the part of men who knew better, and to whom (if to anyone) a frenzied public might listen, has been so common in the eras of mass madness through which we have recently passed, as to compel us to be charitable to the Mathers. And Increase Mather, who had a good share of that wisdom of the serpent denied to his son, took effective measures to stay the frenzy before it destroyed the community. When the court adjourned in September, 1692, twenty persons had been executed, five had been condemned but not executed, one hundred and fifty persons were in prison awaiting trial, and

---

[18] Cotton Mather's letter to one of the judges, John Richards, 'most humbly' begging him not to 'lay more stresse upon pure Spectre testimony than it will bear' is printed in 4 *Coll. M.H.S.*, VIII, 392. The date is May 31, 1692. Cf. C. K. Shipton, in *The American Historical Review*, XL (1935), 464–466.

[19] J. G. Palfrey, *History of New England*, IV (1875), 130–131.

[20] Cotton Mather, *Diary*, I, 150–151.

at least two hundred more had been accused.[21] Following the history of the delusion in England, there was every reason to expect that the vicious circle would widen, until the victims were numbered by the hundreds, and not a mere score. In August, 1692, a group of seven ministers met with Increase Mather at Cambridge to discuss the trials. They decided to make an effort to rule out spectral evidence, and sent to New York to ask the opinion of the ministers there. The New York parsons, French Protestant and Dutch Reformed, replied urging circumspection. Mather then drew up a treatise to guide the court if and when it reassembled; and the book later printed as "Cases of Conscience concerning Evil Spirits" was the result. In this treatise, written with a care and caution that may deceive a hasty reader, they spoke so firmly and conclusively against the use that the court had made of spectral evidence that those in power had to listen. While still in manuscript the treatise was laid before a ministers' meeting in October, and then, signed by Mather and thirteen other ministers, sent up to Governor Phips. The Governor, anxious to do what was right, then dissolved the special court, and ordered spectral evidence to be ruled out by Massachusetts courts in future. Without spectral evidence, there were no more condemnations. As the Governor wrote to the home government, 'The stop put to the first method of proceedings hath dissipated the blak cloud that threatened this Province with destruccion.'[22] Nor did Increase Mather consider his work

finished until he had visited in prison some of the persons who under terror had confessed witchcraft, and obtained recantation from eight of them. No more people were executed or even tried as witches in New England; although one was condemned to death in England as late as 1712, and executions went on in Continental countries until the end of the eighteenth century.

Cotton Mather, too, made partial reparation for his earlier cowardice and his part in urging the execution of George Burroughs, against whom he appears to have had an inveterate malice, by preventing a witchcraft outbreak in Boston. Two serving wenches in Boston, who appear to have resented the fact that the Salem Village girls were getting all the publicity, tried to put Boston on the witchcraft map in 1692 and 1693 by simulating the same symptoms. Cotton Mather never gave them a chance to get a following, or to bring the case before the courts. First one and then the other were taken home with him for treatment; and after they had become bored with being prayed over by a married minister, who was interested only in their souls, they consented to be cured. As in the Goodwin case, Cotton Mather was careful not to divulge the names of those whom the girls accused of bewitching them, lest Boston catch the madness.[23]

21 Palfrey, *op. cit.*, IV, 110. But T. J. Holmes, *Increase Mather: A Bibliography of His Works* (Cleveland, 1931), I, 120, gives 52 as the number in jail.

22 Quoted in T. J. Holmes, *op. cit.*, I, 128, where (pp. 115–134) the whole question of Mather's influence on the proceedings is ably discussed.

23 *The Memorial History of Boston*, II, 148–157; and see Cotton Mather's *Diary*, index under Margaret Rule, and *Narratives of Witchcraft*, pp. 255–287. Professor Burr, in his introduction and notes to the Rule case, puts on Mather's actions, the (it seems to me) totally unwarranted construction that he was moved solely by a desire for notoriety, and to save his own skin, in case the wench accused him of witchcraft. Cotton's *Wonders of the Invisible World* (Boston, 1693) is also an article in the common indictment of him; but a careful reading of the book (which it seldom obtains) will convince any fair-minded reader that it was intended as a warning against

So ended this terrible scourge. Relatively speaking, the Salem witchcraft frenzy was but a small incident in the history of a great superstition. It will always be a blot upon New England because the members of her governing class, especially the judges, did not earlier take a firm stand that would have prevented a mischief. Yet we cannot close even this brief account of the affair unless we relate the sequel, without precedent in the annals of witchcraft. Almost everyone concerned in the accusations and the prosecution, including the ringleaders of the 'afflicted children,' but with the notable exception of Lieutenant-Governor Stoughton, afterwards confessed their error, begged forgiveness of their neighbors, and, as far as in them lay, made reparation. Twenty years after, in consequence of a movement begun by the aged Michael Wigglesworth, the legislature annulled the convictions, reversed the attainders, and granted indemnities to the victims' heirs.[24] The story of this tragedy, in which science joined hands with superstition, may close with mention of that memorable winter's day of 1697, in the Old South Meeting-house, Boston, when Samuel Sewall, former member of the witchcraft court, rose in his pew and stood with bowed head while the minister read his retraction and confession of sin:

Samuel Sewall . . . being sensible, that as to the Guilt contracted upon the opening of the late Commission of Oyer and Terminer at Salem, . . . he is, upon many accounts,

more concerned than any that he knows of Desires to take the Blame and shame of it, asking pardon of men, and especially desiring prayers that God . . . would pardon that sin and all other his sins; and . . . Not Visit the sin of him, or of any other, upon himself, or any of his, nor upon the Land.[25]

* * *

The English puritans who emigrated to New England in the 1630's intended, and in great measure succeeded, in transmitting European civilization to the New World. Realizing that all departments of life not directly useful or absolutely necessary were apt to be sloughed off in a struggle with the wilderness, anticipating that intellectual degeneracy would lead to spiritual decay, they made great sacrifices to transplant the apparatus of civilized life and learning: a university college, grammar schools, elementary schools, printing press, and libraries. The puritan creed, an intellectualized form of Christianity that steered a middle course between a passive acceptance of ecclesiastical authority on the one hand and ignorant emotionalism on the other, stimulated mental activity on the part of those who professed it. The ministers, the most learned class in the colony, maintained an open-minded and receptive attitude toward the significant scientific discoveries of their century, and young college graduates made some attempt at dispelling superstition by their popular essays in the almanacs. The 'warfare between science and theology' found no battleground in New England, where the clergy were leaders in liberalism and enlightenment, purveyors of new learning to the people.[26] Although the clergy

further shedding of innocent blood, not as an incitement to fresh frenzies. The most that can be alleged is that Cotton would have been wiser not to have written it.

24 Palfrey, IV, 116–117; cf. Sibley, *Harvard Graduates*, IV, 231, for the work of a very young minister, Joseph Green, in bringing peace to Salem Village. Wigglesworth's letter is in 4 *Coll. M.H.S.*, VIII, 645–646.

25 Sewall, *Diary*, I, 445.

26 See facts mentioned by C. K. Shipton in *The American Historical Review*, XL (1935), 463–464.

did attempt to canalize the popular mind into religious ways, and to a remarkable degree succeeded, their conception of religion was sufficiently broad and stimulating to provide a dynamic motive for the intellectual movement in New England, and to give colonial literature a certain unity and dignity. In spite of the emphasis on a religion derived from the Bible, the best of the ancient classics were included in the school and college curricula. Contemporary English literature was imported and read; young men showed an appreciation of the humane English poetry of the Elizabethan era, and wrote imitations of it as best they could.

In providing institutions that later generations could put to new uses, the New Englanders were more successful than in actual intellectual production. No lasting books were written, no new or significant ideas were worked out on New England soil; but three institutions of lasting significance for American life were firmly established: the college, the public-school system, and the Congregational Church. A veneration for learning, a respect for the humanities, and a habit of considering values other than material had been so firmly established among the ruling class of the New England people by 1701, that they were as well prepared as any people in the world to be quickened by new ideas, and to play their part in the coming drama of the Rights of Man.

Thus, the story of the intellectual life of New England in the seventeenth century is not merely that of a people bravely and successfully endeavoring to keep up the standards of civilization in the New World; it is one of the principal approaches to the social and intellectual history of the United States. Primitive New England is a puritan pronaos to the American mind of the nineteenth century, and of today.

Marion L. Starkey:

THE DEVIL AND COTTON MATHER *

WHAT was the devil? To the Puritan the question was no less important than the question, what is God. A surprising variety of answers were possible. Some in Massachusetts were still reading an English best seller two decades old, John Milton's *Paradise Lost*, in which the poet in defeat and blindness had all unconsciously created Satan in his own image, doomed, but not without his grandeur. Such a being could be abhorred but not despised; one might pity, even respect the enemy of mankind. In his contest with Omnipotence he showed

* [The Salem witchcraft of 1692, which resulted in the execution of twenty "witches," has been advanced as an example of the evil effect of the Puritans' ideological intensities. A pack of teen-aged girls oppressed, it is thought, by the religious and moral dogmas of Massachusetts Bay,

Reprinted from *The Devil in Massachusetts* by Marion L. Starkey, by permission of Alfred A. Knopf, Inc. Copyright 1949 by Alfred A. Knopf, Inc.

a perverse nobility of spirit; there was something almost Promethean in the tragic Satan who from hell defied the lightning of heaven and reached out to make mankind his own.

Yet how far was such a concept understood in provincial Massachusetts whose own tastes were represented not by the organ music of Milton's blank verse but by the jigging and jingling of Wigglesworth's *Day of Doom?* Certainly Cotton Mather, who had his own copy of *Paradise Lost,* did not associate Satan with the grandeur of lost but not ignoble causes. His Satan had more the spirit of the poltergeist, or of the comic devil of the early miracle plays. The fellow was ubiquitous, and as such damnably dangerous and eternally a nuisance, but as little dignified as the worm that eats up the garden.

Still a third concept was possible, the strange Adversary who presented himself before God in the time of Job and was received with courteous attention. What manner of devil was this who did not stoop to laying petty ambush for his enemy, but came openly into God's presence to challenge him; and what meaning could be read into God's acceptance of a challenge from such a source? Could it be that such was the omnipotence of God that the very devil worked for him to examine the hearts of men and test the

limits of their faith? Was it even possible that God made use of the devil to bring a new thing on earth, that out of ill good would come?

Yet what good would come out of what the devil had done in Massachusetts? The phase of the colony's martyrdom had been not single but multiple. Not the witchcraft only but the new charter had delivered the faithful into the devil's hand. Now that people outside the faith could vote and shape the course of government, the power of theocracy had been forever broken. No longer would it be possible to get rid of perversely creative minds — the Ann Hutchinsons and Roger Williamses — by exile or death. Demoniac energies had been loosed now, and God alone could foresee the outcome. Was it possible that what the devil had promised William Barker of Andover would come to pass under God's providence, that there would be no more sin or shame or judgment, "that all men should be equal and live bravely"?

Well, it was God's will. God had delivered them if not to the devil, at least to an adversary. God save the Commonwealth of Massachusetts.

If symptoms of diabolism had faded at last in Salem Village — so odd a site for God to choose as the battleground between hell and heaven — there was dev-

began to find an outlet in emotional orgies during which they expressed fantasies founded on the current religious belief in the devil and his ability to enter into the shape of mortals and compel them to do his bidding. The girls accused aged, often unpopular members of the community, of appearing before them as agents of the devil and persecuting them. Their hysteria spread through the community; neighbor turned against neighbor, and decent men and women were sent to prison and the gallows, convicted merely on the evidence of anyone at all that they had appeared spectrally as tormenting witches. Finally, after accusations had spread to most unlikely people, including even the wife of Governor Phips, the

good sense of a few began to assert itself. The fear that skepticism might only invite retaliation in the form of accusation of witchcraft against the skeptic was overcome. Thomas Brattle, a prominent Boston merchant, scientist, and churchman, circulated a letter denouncing the executions as based on gossip and the irresponsible pretensions of afflicted adolescents. In January, 1693, Governor William Phips pardoned those who had not been executed and ordered their release. But for some the battle against the devil was by no means over. The role played by Cotton Mather in the whole affair and the significance of the aftermath in Boston is the subject of the chapter which follows. Ed.]

iltry aplenty in Boston. Even while the judges were dismissing the witches, Cotton Mather's own wife, she who had once had to smother a laugh at the sight of diabolic manifestation as observed in the person of little Martha Goodwin, had been affrighted on her porch by a diabolic vision and had in consequence given birth to a malformed, short-lived child.

And as if that were not enough, Mather himself, because of his charitable interest in certain afflicted maids of Boston, was about to be given to drink of the vinegar of mockery by what he called "the witlings of the coffee houses." The devil had lately discovered to Boston a new brew which sharpened the wit and incited it to skepticism. Here in the waning days of the witchcraft were wont to sit several of the devil's own who made it their business to keep a derisive eye on the current activities of Cotton Mather and to publish them to the town.

Until lately there had been little occasion to connect the younger Mather with the witchcraft. He who had been so active in the Glover affair, and whose record of the case had helped prepare Massachusetts for the new outbreak, had nevertheless remained surprisingly aloof from the latter. Not that the aloofness had been by intention; it was simply a matter of living far from Salem and having much to detain him in Boston.

Early in the day he had written the Salem authorities offering to receive any six girls into his home for observation and treatment; had the magistrates responded it is probable that they would have exchanged a major calamity for yet another quaint, archaic monograph. The segregation of the girls would have served to localize the psychic infection, and the girls themselves, exposed to the wayward streak of poetry in Mather's composition, would almost certainly have found their fantasies deflected to the more normal preoccupations of adolescence. They would, in short, like a large proportion of the female members of his congregation at any given time, have fallen in love with him. Infatuation is not any guarantee against hysteria; quite the contrary. But in this case such a development might have diverted the antics of the girls to less malignant forms. Young Ann Putnam might, like Martha Goodwin, have ridden an airy horse up and down the stairs and into the pastor's study, to find her catharsis there rather than before the gallows.

It had not been given Mather thus to experiment; he had watched the case from afar and had only thrice taken positive action. One of these occasions had been his drafting of the advice of the ministers to the judges, cautioning them against too great reliance on spectral evidence, though praising their zeal. Even before then Mather had unofficially written in the same vein to Judge John Richards, not only warning him against spectral evidence but against uncritical acceptance of such confessions as might come from a "delirious brain or a discontented heart." He specifically denounced torture as a means of getting confessions.

His only dramatic intervention in the witchcraft had been the speech he had made to the crowd at the hanging of Burroughs.* This speech was the only real complaint that his enemies could make against him. There were some who

* [At the scaffold Burroughs, a minister accused of being the ringleader of the witches, had been allowed to speak and had created such a favorable impression that the crowd made a move to rescue him. Mather, who had ridden out to see the hanging, rose in his stirrups and warned the crowd that they were being taken in by just another of the devil's tricks. They were quieted and the execution proceeded. Ed.]

thought that Mather had shown small charity to a fellow minister in his hour of need. Yet not much could be fairly made of the incident. Had not Mather spoken another must, for the crowd before the gallows was fast deteriorating into a mob. Mather who had seen mobs in Boston in 1689 had acted instinctively and without premeditation to do what was necessary to quiet this one. Control of the crowd and not slander of Burroughs had been his purpose.

In any case the incident was now well in the past. It would not have been held a serious count against Mather, nor could his name have been fairly connected with the witchcraft but for what happened after it was all over.

On September 22, 1692, a kind of council-of-war had been called at Samuel Sewall's house in Boston. Present were Samuel's brother Stephen of Salem, Captain John Higginson, John Hathorne, William Stoughton and Cotton Mather. The subject under discussion was the propriety of making public some of the evidence in the witch trials. Not since Lawson's *Brief and True Narrative* of last spring had there been any authoritative published statement, and the latter had been written months in advance of the sitting of the Court of Oyer and Terminer. Now with so much irresponsible talk going on, it seemed clear that the time had come for an official report on what the judges had accomplished for Massachusetts. It would be an interim report. As of this date the judges expected to go forward with the trials in October. In spite of the rising tide of protest none could know that the seven women and one man who that day hung on the gallows in Salem would be the very last witches to hang in Massachusetts.

Mather stood ready to take on this assignment, and had been anticipating it for some time. To this end he had been accumulating some of his own sermons, notably his "Hortatory and Necessary Address" with its charge upon the conscience of New England. "'Tis our Worldliness, our Formality, our Sensuality and our Iniquity that has helped this letting of the Devils in." In addition he had been after Stephen Sewall to copy out such of the documents in Salem as could be used in a history of the witchcraft. Some of this material — not quite so much as he had hoped — was now available. If it was the will of his colleagues he would gladly do his best with a subject, which had been, he modestly reminded them, "sometimes counted not unworthy the pen, even of a king."

Whatever the faults of the younger Mather, procrastination was not one of them. By early October when Phips returned, the manuscript was not only complete, awaiting the latter's approval, but had already had some circulation among dignitaries of the colony. That he had also done his work well, had achieved what could be regarded as the authoritative version of the affair, was indicated not only by a laudatory preface by Stoughton, but by the fact that Sir William borrowed whole paragraphs for incorporation into his first report to England.

Phips did not, however, encourage publication. Brattle's letter, which denounced the entire premises of the trials, was circulating as far and as fast as Mather's defense. At a time of such diversity of opinion so hotly expressed the governor found it wise to suppress any publicity whatsoever. It was not until 1693 when the trials had been resumed on a new basis and the "general jail delivery" begun that he judged it wise to let Mather publish his *Wonders of the Invisible World.*

Mather's narrative was the nearest equivalent Massachusetts was to get to a full newspaper report of the mysterious events in court. The public fell on it with avidity and got their money's worth. Mingled in with sermons and philosophizings, Mather had presented a full and accurate account of the examination and trials of five representative witches, George Burroughs, Bridget Bishop, Susanna Martin, Elizabeth How, and Martha Carrier. He had followed the records in painstaking detail, summarizing competently when he did not quote in full. Not even his worst enemies were ever to find fault with his court reporting, and compared with the chapbooks of such cases put out to entertain the English public, it was a journalistic masterpiece.

Yet this document, so well planned and executed, so invaluable to the historian, was to serve the reputation of Mather ill. It had two conspicuous defects: its omissions and its tone. Those who really knew the trials read a significance into the fact that Mather had carefully avoided several of their most embarrassing aspects, Rebecca Nurse's brief acquittal, the powerful reasoning of John Procter and Mary Esty.* The avoidance, to be sure, was by no means necessarily Mather's doing; what to include and what to omit had certainly been one of

* [Rebecca Nurse, grand old matriarch of the Nurse clan, known as a pious Puritan mother, had been declared not guilty of witchcraft. Judge Stoughton had asked the jury to reconsider, and it changed its verdict under the stress of courtroom clamor and renewed fits on the part of the accusing girls. Procter and Mary Esty had asked at their trials for fairer proceedings, removal if necessary to a community where passions were less inflamed, and had protested their innocence and the illegality of spectral evidence, all to no avail. Ed.]

the subjects of discussion at the editorial meeting at Sewall's house. These circumstances could not, however, negate the fact that Mather had lent his hand to fabricating that most dangerous of falsehoods, the half truth.

The tone of the book was another thing again, and wholly Mather's. It suggested that the Dutch divines had spoken against spectral evidence in vain, and that Mather himself in recommending caution in this direction had not meant it. For he had written throughout in a spirit of childlike, marveling credulity.

Yet how could Mather, given his temperament, have written otherwise of his witches? As well ask Shakespeare to revise *Macbeth* without mentioning the Weird Sisters, or Milton to erase all reference to Satan in *Paradise Lost* as to ask Mather to do other than what he had done. There was in him much of the artist, and artistry in his austere position in theocratic Massachusetts found only such wayward expression as this. To such a temperament — and some of the afflicted girls probably resembled him in this — the details of the witchcraft, of horns that sounded across Essex County at midnight, the airborne excursions to Parris' pasture, the folklore that gaudily embroidered the life of Susanna Martin, were less a horror and an abomination than part of the suppressed color and drama of life. Mather's righteous indignation that such things could be was unconsciously submerged in the thrill of having been present as spectator at a collision between heaven and hell. The witchcraft was one experience that Mather would not willingly have foregone; it was the scarlet thread drawn through the drab of New England homespun.

But men who had been painfully involved in the crisis were little likely to respond to so artless and unconsciously poetic a viewpoint. What impressed them was that in his zeal for discovering witches an eminent Boston divine had stultified his capacity to see human beings and their very real agonies, that in short, to judge by the tone of his record, he had learned nothing at all from experience. So far as he was concerned, the delirium might begin again full force tomorrow.

Indeed the delusion had by no means spent itself. While the afflicted of Andover and Salem were falling one by one into silence, dampened by the lack of a responsive audience, new voices were being heard in Boston. To two of these Mather was giving all the attention he could spare from his parochial duties. He was, in fact, launched on a whole new cycle of psychic research.

The first case to come to his attention was that of Mercy Short, seventeen-year-old servant maid of Boston, recently back from captivity among the Indians, who, as natural creatures of the devil, had probably had not too wholesome an influence on the girl. It was Mercy who in the course of a call on the Boston Prison in the summer of 1692 had mocked Sarah Good's plea for tobacco and had been afflicted since.

One would have supposed that the hanging of Sarah would have released Mercy, but not at all. Sarah must have delegated the torture of the girl to her surviving confederates, for it went right on through the summer and fall and became a favorite subject of speculation among the frequenters of the coffee houses. On December 4 Mercy achieved the attention of Cotton Mather by falling into such convulsions during a sermon that she had to be carried out. Naturally

Mather looked her up afterwards, both he and a "little company of praying neighbors." He had long been itching to study at close range the type of case responsible for the Salem outbreak; now at last he had one in his own precinct.

From his interviews with this medium he got a first hand description of the devil, "a short and black man — a Wretch no taller than an ordinary Walking Staff; he was not a Negro but of a Tawney or an Indian color; he wore a high crowned hat with straight hair; and he had one Cloven Foot." The eyes of this creature flamed unbearably, resembling according to Mercy, the glass ball of the lantern Mather took with him through the dim streets of Boston on his nocturnal rambles.

Sometimes Mercy's affliction took the form of long fasts, during which she could force herself to take nothing but hard cider. Sometimes she was seared by flames, and her visitors could smell the brimstone and see the burns on Mercy's flesh, though "as 'tis the strange property of many witch marks," these were "cured in perhaps less than a minute." Sometimes the devil forced white liquid down her throat. Sometimes she had fits of wild frolic when she was deaf to all prayers.

It was not for want of name calling on Mercy's part that these investigations did not result in arrests. She cried out against all sorts of people, especially some with whom she had recently quarreled. But Mather, acting with a discretion for which he was not to be thanked, decided that most of these were devil's delusions and charged his "praying company" not to report them. Among Mercy's more oblique accusations was Mather himself; this fact gave him more gratification than otherwise, for he gathered from the context that the devil feared and hated him more than any other minister in New England, a very pretty compliment.

Mercy, responding to fasting, prayer, and the invisible ministrations of an angel who sometimes fended the devils off, finally came out of her trance in March, 1693, and Mather wrote up his observations under the title of *A Brand Pluck'd out of the Burning*. Somehow he did not publish it. The jail delivery was in progress, and friends and relatives of released witches would not appreciate yet another starry-eyed report of this sort, especially so soon after the *Wonders*, from whose philosophies some of them were cringing. Or perhaps it was the development of Mercy herself which restrained him. The sad truth was that when the devil was cast out of her, seven others took its place, these being devils of the more common and carnal sort. Martyrs are impressive in the long run only when they are also saints; since Mercy was plainly nothing of the sort, Mather's pious account of her sufferings would be oddly received in Boston's coffee houses, places much more productive of skepticism than the ale houses had ever been. Mather did not risk it.

Mather was, however, by no means done with the devil. In September, 1693, he made a trip to Salem to get "furniture" for the completion of the work now nearest to his heart, his *Magnalia Christi Americana*. This was to be his epic in somewhat the same way that *Paradise Lost* was Milton's. His purpose was cognate, though whereas Milton had undertaken to justify the ways of God to man, Mather would seek to justify the ways of man to God, particularly man as represented by the leaders of Puritan theocracy. He would eschew the sonorities of

blank verse for the plainer sense of English prose, albeit richly embellished by latinisms, and the somber glory of such characters as Beelzebub and Lucifer for the more unassuming personnel to be found in New England parsonages; the *Magnalia* was indeed to be primarily a history of the churches in New England. Lucifer, however, would not be ignored in Mather's work; he would again give himself the luxury of describing the Fiend's descent on Salem Village.

To such an end he came to Salem. He delivered two sermons and between them pursued his inquiries. He was much interested in a Mrs. Carver and her viewpoint on late events. This lady was in direct communication with "shining spirits" who told her that "a new storm of witchcraft would fall upon the country and chastise the iniquity that was used in the wilful smothering and covering of the last."

This news Mather received about as a general might receive intelligence that he would soon be called upon to march again. There had indeed been something abrupt, something questionable about the end of the witchcraft. The case had not been so much disposed of as allowed to collapse. It was as if an army of occupation had been called home without awaiting the signing of a peace treaty. It would be little wonder if the devil were to begin a new assault against a people so little capable of sustained effort.

These reflections were reinforced by evidence that the devil was interfering directly in his own affairs. He had prepared two sermons to deliver in Salem and the devil stole them both. Luckily he was able to give them from memory "so the devil got nothing." The story did not end there. When he got home to Boston he found that affliction had started again in his own neighborhood in the person of another seventeen-year-old, one Margaret Rule. From Margaret's lips he learned what had happened in Salem. The eight spectral shapes that tormented her had stolen his sermons and were bragging about it. Yet it was not given to creatures covenanted to the devil to keep a hold on a thing so holy as a sermon by Cotton Mather. In October the spirits relaxed their grip and dropped the missing manuscripts leaf by leaf about the streets of Lynn. Every page was recovered in a perfect state of preservation.

After such portents Mather could not deny his time and prayers to the new victim of the invisible world. Margaret was indeed a pitiful case. Her present physical tortures had been preceded by a spiritual phase in which she was prey to a belief that she was damned. Now she was the victim of witches who desired her to sign the Book. She was resisting heroically and before a cloud of witnesses. For Margaret was yet another who had had to be carried shrieking from meeting; since that had first happened on September 10, she had become the major theatrical attraction in Boston. If Mather wanted to minister to her privately he must first clear the room of a company — by no means a praying company — of thirty or forty spectators. Frequently he did not take this precaution, with the result that a fraction of the population of Boston was entertained not only by the antics of Margaret but by the measures taken by Mather to exorcize her demons.

Margaret's affliction had begun with an involuntary fast. For nine days her teeth had set against food, though occasionally it was possible to get her mouth open just wide enough to admit a sip of rum. ("That's the devil all over," commented a seaman.) Sometimes it was the devil who forced open her mouth in order to pour scalding brimstone down her throat so that people in the room could hardly bear the smell of the stuff or the sound of the girl's screams.

Marvels happened right under the eyes of the beholders. Some of them saw the woman stuck full of pins. Six men signed affidavits that they had seen her pulled to the ceiling by invisible hands and that it took their concerted might to pull her back to bed again. Mather himself once made a grab for something stirring on her pillow and felt an imp in his hand, tangible and yet invisible, and so startling in that combination that he let it get away.

She dreamed dreams and saw visions. She forecast the drowning of a young man and exactly as she spoke it happened — almost; that is, by God's providence the man wasn't actually drowned but was fished out of the water into which sundry devils had impelled him to leap. She saw the thieving of an old man's will. She saw the faces of her tormenters, or anyway of some of them, particularly that of an evil old woman who had been taken in the recent witchcraft and incontinently released again when the judges lost their heart for proper prosecution. Some witches she could not identify because they, having learned a thing or two, now went about their business veiled. Veiled or no, when Mather got to her, he prevailed on her to "forbear blazing their names lest any good person come to suffer any blast of reputation." He was willing that she name them to him privately and was reassured, for they were "the sort of wretches who for these many years have given over as violent presumption of witchcraft as perhaps any creatures yet living on this earth." Even so he did not report them.

He got small thanks for his self-sacrificing labors in behalf of Margaret Rule. His efforts had been observed by a motley company come off the streets of Boston to see the show, merchants, seamen, scholars, goodwives, everybody. These behaved decorously enough in his presence and on the whole he thought it well that a variety of observers witness the agonies of the girl the better to combat the skepticism of the coffee houses. What he did not know was that one of these "coffee house witlings" had not only got in with the rest but was taking copious notes of the seances and preparing to publish.

This observer was Robert Calef, an obscure merchant of Boston. He was a friend of Thomas Brattle and agreed with the skeptical viewpoint expressed in Brattle's letter, and had therefore come to watch Mather in non-too-reverent a frame of mind. What his cold eye noted in the afflicted Margaret was her craving for the attentions of men. She visibly liked being stroked across face and naked breast and belly by the Mathers, father and son, this being a kind of laying on of hands by which they tried to relieve her, but let a woman touch her and she cried out sharply, "Don't you meddle with me!"

When the ministers withdrew, Margaret told the women to clear out altogether, saying "that the company of men was not offensive to her, and having hold of the hand of a young man said to have been her sweetheart . . . she pulled him again into his seat saying he should not go tonight."

Six days later Calef found her enjoying what Mather had explained to observers as "her laughing time; she must laugh

now." Mather having already gone for the evening, she was free to make eyes at yet another young man and to fuss with her attendants because they "did not put her on a clean cap but let her lie so like a beast, saying she would lose her fellows."

There was talk, to be sure, about her frightful affliction earlier in the day, and there were symptoms of a recurrence when one or two of the women got a whiff of brimstone. Everyone sniffed with them, but Calef and others couldn't pick up the scent and said so. The women became less sure of themselves; they could smell something, they said; they were not sure what.

Calef, in short, was less than impressed with the martyred Margaret. Even less had he been impressed in the still recent past by what he called a "Bigotted Zeal stirring up a Blind and most Bloody Rage" against innocent people by such media as these. He resented the credulous interest of the Mathers, particularly Cotton; this sort of thing had led to public disaster only two years earlier. Calef did not propose to stand by and watch the engineering of a second outbreak. Accordingly he copied out his notes and let them circulate from hand to hand.

Never in his life had Mather been so rudely handled or so affronted as he was by the talk to which these notes gave rise. He was enraged by the description of his stroking the half-naked Margaret so as "to make people believe a Smutty thing of me." His first impulse was to bring suit for "scandalous libel"; his second not to risk so public an appearance on so delicate an issue. The warrant was issued against Calef, but when the latter appeared before court, none came against him and the case was dismissed.

The larger case was not at all dismissed, however. The controversy between minister and merchant went on for years and culminated at the turn of the century in a book called *More Wonders of the Invisible World,* a work by Calef with the involuntary collaboration of Mather and a probable but disguised contribution by Brattle. Its core was the later witch writings of Mather, including his unpublished account of Margaret Rule. To this Calef added his own appendix to Mather's *Wonders,* furnishing full details on cases which Mather had neglected, notably that of Rebecca Nurse, and adding reports by such survivors as the Carys and John Alden.

Its publication was one of the most afflicting things that had ever happened to Mather, his sorrow's crown of sorrow. And indeed, though Calef's work was a valuable addition to the history of witchcraft, it did inflict an injustice on Mather in connecting his name inseparably with a tragedy with which he actually had had little to do.

Increase Mather, who himself had drawn Calef's fire, owing to his proposal to New England ministers in 1695 that they continue to collect "Remarkables," among them evidence of the agency of the invisible world, stood loyally by his son and made a spectacle of the infamy of the book — or so the story goes — by having it burned in the Harvard Yard. This fine symbolic gesture had oddly little effect in preventing its circulation.

Margaret Rule had in the meantime come out of her fits long since. It was well that Calef never heard of her last seance with Mather, for during it she dreamily named the wizard whose Shape was currently afflicting her, and it was none other than Cotton's.

Mather was terrified. Superstition played little part in his fright, nor did he anticipate taking a place by Burroughs on the gallows. What unmanned him was the derision of the coffee houses if this accusation ever got around.

Heroic measures were necessary, heights of prayer to which he had never won before. He won them now. Finally, after Mather had spent several hours in the dust before his God, the "shining spirit" that had intermittently appeared to Margaret came again and informed her that Mather was now her father in Christ and that through God's providence he had saved her. The angel also opened her eyes to the actual demons crowded around her. They were rather pitiful; the devil himself stood over them lashing them to further effort, for all the world like an overseer whipping his slaves. Indeed the demons were fainting under the punishment and under the strain of their hopeless endeavor. At last they cried out to Margaret, "Go and the devil go with you. We can do no more." Then they fled the place. Nor did they come again, at least in that guise. Margaret's affliction and Boston's best show were both a thing of the past; hereafter Margaret had no more difficulty in getting privacy for her interviews with her "fellows."

Mather for his part learned to keep strictly away from her. His "spiritual daughter" did not turn out to be a very nice girl.

Kenneth B. Murdock:

THE PURITAN LITERARY ATTITUDE

THERE is nothing in the religious literature of Puritan New England to match the richest pages of the great seventeenth-century Anglicans. It is a far cry from the poems of Herbert and Vaughan to the verses of Anne Bradstreet and the jog-trot measures of Michael Wigglesworth's *Day of Doom*, or from the magnificence of Jeremy Taylor's prose or Donne's to the best that the colonists wrote. But this is not to say that that best had no merit. There are many flashes of poetry, many passages of eloquent prose, and, throughout, a style that rarely descends to mere tame mediocrity. The work of the best writers in colonial New England shows that they wanted to write well as one way of serving God, and reflects both their zeal and their concern for fundamental stylistic values.

The more this work is examined in the light of the handicaps the colonists faced and the standards they set for themselves, the more impressive it becomes. In seventy years they made Boston second only to London in the English-speaking world as a center for the publishing and marketing of books, and they produced a body of writing greater in quantity and quality than that of any other colonial community in modern history. Its merits may escape him who reads as he runs, but to the more patient it may offer fuller insight into the best qualities of the Puritan settlers and their eagerness to find an adequate literary creed for pious purposes. The study of it may encourage a valuable humility in the face of the problem of religious expression as it exists even in our own times.

It is important first of all to realize that the American Puritan who wanted to be an artist in words — or, to put it more explicitly, who wanted to communicate his thoughts and emotion to others in such a way as to convince and move them — was faced by certain tangible handicaps. He was a colonist, and New England, compared to London, a wilderness. George Herbert in his quiet Wiltshire parish, John Donne in the deanery of St. Paul's, or Jeremy Taylor in the calm retirement of the Golden Grove, enjoyed advantages denied the pioneer Bostonian. They had within reach — at the most only a few days' journey away — the best libraries and the best intellectual society of which England could boast. Their place as scholars and artists was recognized; they could count on readers and hearers able to appreciate fully not only the substance of what they wrote but whatever literary skill they showed in it. They might be mystics or rationalists, high-church men or liberals, Calvinists or Arminians, and there were enough like-minded readers to welcome them. They might use the classics or the church fathers, experiment with all the devices of rhetoric, and seek out new images for their ideas, secure in the knowledge that learned readers trained in an artistic tradition would acclaim

From *Literature and Theology in Colonial New England* by Kenneth B. Murdock. Harvard University Press, 1949. Reprinted by permission.

their successes. But the New England colonist had no library to compare with those to be found in London; his audience, although eager, was limited in its tastes and inexperienced in literary niceties. If the colonial writer yearned for "good talk" or lively debates on literary problems he had to choose his companions from a very few, and some of those were sure to be separated from him by hours of travel on a difficult or dangerous road. He did read and he did write, but he could do so only as the exigencies of life in a pioneer community left him leisure. And even when Boston grew to a town of comfortable size and colonial life became relatively easy, the learned man and would-be artist was almost inevitably also a man whose political or religious duties engrossed much of his time. Anyone who can picture the hardships and practical complications they had to meet will be more inclined to wonder that Puritan writers wrote as much and as well as they did than to cavil at the fact that their work sometimes shows signs of crudity or haste.

No great artist, however, has ever been made or marred by the purely material conditions under which he worked. Geniuses have flourished in attics and mere scribblers in great libraries. The Puritan writer had many concrete obstacles to surmount, but his stylistic practice and his successes and failures were determined not so much by the fact that the ink sometimes froze in his inkwell as he worked, or by anything else in his environment, as by the ideas he held and those he rejected. These ideas, theological and philosophic, affected more profoundly than any material circumstance what he wrote and how.

To begin with, he was a Puritan — that is, an extreme Protestant. He found in Scripture no authority for vestments or "the painted texts" with which George Herbert thought the parson should adorn his church. From this the strict Puritan concluded that such things were improper, since God would have asked for them had he wished them. The fact that Catholics and high-church Anglicans alike used incense, organ music, and other means of sensuous appeal in worship was, for the Puritan, proof of their sinful neglect of Scripture. So also in literature. Catholic writing as a whole was evil; so was such Anglican literature as seemed to him unsound in doctrine. Therefore he not unreasonably linked his distrust of ideas that seemed to him unworthy of a good Protestant with a dislike for the style in which those ideas were most commonly set forth.

The dislike is easy to illustrate. John Cotton, for example, while he was an Anglican at Cambridge University, was famous for brilliant sermons, "elegantly and oratoriously performed," and was "applauded by all the gallant scholars," but when he became a Puritan he chose instead to preach in a "plain, honest" style.[1] One of his Puritan biographers praises him for giving up the "florid strains" which "extremely recommended him unto *the most,* who relished the *wisdom of words* above the *words of wisdom*" and admired "pompous eloquence."[2] Thomas Hooker of New England is clearly referring to the Anglican preachers of the early seventeenth century when he says, "I have sometime admired . . . why a company of Gentlemen, Yeomen, and poore women, that are scarcely able to know their A.B.C. . . .

[1] Samuel Whiting's life of John Cotton, printed in Alexander Young, *Chronicles of the First Planters of Massachusetts Bay* (Boston, 1846), pp. 421–422.

[2] Cotton Mather, *Magnalia Christi Americana,* book III, part I, chapter 1, paragraph 4. I have quoted the text of the 1855 Hartford edition.

have a Minister to speake Latine, Greeke, and Hebrew, and to use the Fathers, when it is certaine, they know nothing at all." The result is, Hooker thinks, that they "goe to hell hood-winckt, never awakened."[3] Richard Mather, another pioneer New England minister, "studiously avoided obscure phrases, Exotick Words, or an unnecessary citation of Latine Sentences, which some men addict themselves to the use of . . . This humble man" looked "upon the affectation of such things . . . to savour of Carnal wisdome."[4] Still another New Englander, Ebenezer Turell, writing in the eighteenth century but echoing an old refrain, says that a minister gives offense if he uses "the Jargon of Logic and Metaphysicks" or amuses his audience with foreign names "or soars above them in Flights of Poetry and Flourishes of rhetorick."[5] The references in such passages as these are clearly to common features of the style of many Anglican sermons.

All this is related, of course, to the difference between the Catholic and Protestant attitudes on the use of sensuous material in religious literature. The settlers of Massachusetts Bay found little room in their scheme of things for the graphic arts, or for any art which seemed only to please the senses. As Perry Miller puts it:

The Puritan lived in this world, and tried desperately not to be of it; he followed his calling, plowed his land, laid away his shillings, and endeavored to keep his mind on the future life. He looked upon the physical world as the handiwork of God, and the charms of the universe as His creations, and yet he told himself, "Get thy heart more and more weaned from the Creature, the Creature is empty, its not able to satisfie thee fully, nor make thee happy."[6]

The beauties of the physical world were all too likely to distract men's minds from religious truth or to arouse in them feelings alien to those proper for the study and worship of the divine. . . .

Anglicans and Puritans agreed about the ease with which in worship, prayer, or religious contemplation men's minds might wander away from the spiritual. Where Donne and most English churchmen differed from most Puritans was in the methods by which they tried to hold men's attention. To judge from their practice, the Anglicans and Catholics believed that one reason for using wit and rhetoric and imagery and material which catered to the senses as well as to the intellect in religious writing was that such things served to control the reader's unruly mind. But the Puritan made fewer concessions to human frailty, perhaps because he was more convinced of how frail man is. He kept away from anything, however appealing, that he thought might make men's hearts stray from theological truth and self-forgetful devotion toward pleasantly sensuous reveries on this world. . . .

Still another determining influence on the Puritan artist was his reverence for the Bible. Theologically, of course, he depended on it as the one absolute authority, and in polity and doctrine fol-

[3] Thomas Hooker, *The Soules Preparation for Christ* (London, 1632), p. 66.

[4] Increase Mather, *The Life and Death of . . . Mr. Richard Mather,* reprinted in *Collections of the Dorchester Antiquarian and Historical Society,* no. 3 (Boston, 1850), p. 85.

[5] Ebenezer Turell, *Ministers should carefully avoid giving Offense in any Thing* (Boston, 1740), p. 15.

[6] Perry Miller and Thomas H. Johnson, *The Puritans* (New York, 1938), p. 289.

lowed it, or believed he did, to the letter.
Inevitably, then, when he preached or
wrote on divine themes he tended to
limit his diction, his images, and his literary devices to those which he could find
in Holy Writ. In subject matter too,
obviously what was closest to the Bible
was best. Biblical style was perfect because it was "penned by the Holy
Ghost." It was a style of "great simplicitie and wonderful plainnesse," "un-
polished," avoiding "the flowers of
Rhetoricke," "the goodly ornaments of
humane eloquence," and "wittie sharpe
conceits." "If the Lord had penned y^e
scriptures in such an eloquent stile as
would have ravished the readers with
delight, we would like fooles have stood
admiring at ye curious work of the casket,
and never opened it to look upon the
precious jewel therein contained; and
have bin so much affected with the
words, that in the meane time we would
have neglected the matter."[7] The Puritan's rigid adherence to the literal word
of God, as he understood it, would have
been almost enough in itself to explain
his avoidance of some material commonly
used by Catholic and Anglican writers
and to account for many of the standards
he set for himself both in content and in
style.

The most immediate influence on the
Puritan's literary practice, however, especially in New England, was almost certainly the character of his audience.
Whatever his theories might have been,
it would have been hopeless for him to
try to act on them if the result would not
have won him readers and made them
understand. By and large, the strength
of Puritanism, here and in the mother
country, lay in the plain man, eager for
knowledge, better educated than his

father had been, excited by the possibilities that books seemed to hold, but still
unversed in literature as such and unable
to grasp either the intricate rhetoric of
learned and witty sermons like those of
Lancelot Andrews, or the Latin and
Greek quotations, the allusions, and the
complicated imagery of much of the
great Anglican religious literature of his
time. Especially in preaching, a tradition
had been built up for just such men — a
tradition in which "plainnesse" was a literary virtue. Homeliness of imagery, simplicity of diction, and a constant emphasis on the values most easily recognizable
by honest Englishmen of no pretensions
to critical acumen characterized this
style, and the influence of the audience
in shaping it is patent. John Downame,
an English Puritan, already quoted on
the "simplicitie" and "plainnesse" of the
Bible, wrote in the same passage that
Holy Writ was adapted "to the capacitie
of the most unlearned."[8] The Scriptures,
he continued, "speak in the same manner,
and injoyne the like obedience, to prince
and people, rich and poore, learned and
unlearned, without any difference or
respect of person . . . and therefore . . .
the Lord . . . useth a simple easie stile fit
for the capacitie of all, because it was
for the use of all."[9]

The Puritan in New England did not
believe in political democracy, but he
did believe that religious teaching was a
matter for all men, and he deliberately
directed most of what he wrote at the
whole community. Since most of his fellow colonists were relatively untutored it
was clear that his style must be direct
and simple enough to strike home to
them. There was always St. Paul's re-
minder, "Except ye utter by the tongue

[7] John Downame, *Christian Warfare* (London,
1609), pp. 339, 341, 342.

[8] Downame, p. 339.

[9] Downame, pp. 340–341.

words easy to be understood, how shall it be known what is spoken?"[10]

Scattered everywhere throughout Puritan literature, American and English, are reiterations of the idea that the tastes and aptitudes of simple people must be catered to in religious writing. Richard Baxter once wrote to an Anglican friend, "Had I never been a Pastor nor lived out of a College (and had met with such a taking orator) I might have thought as you do. And had you convert with as many country people as I have done, and such country-people, I think you would have thought as I do."[11] Clearly Baxter was linking "country-people" and their religious needs with Puritanism, and associating Anglicanism with the learned in colleges and those who had not "converst" with humbler folk. He seems to have been right; the extreme Puritanism of his day found its readiest audience among men who pretended to no social or intellectual eminence. Baxter's own poems, he thought, might "profit two sorts, women and vulgar christians and persons in passion and affliction."[12] He knew they would not please the wits, but as a good Puritan he was content to let them go out to help those who were unschooled in poetry but zealous in piety. Richard Mather in the colonies tried in his sermons to avoid certain tricks of style which, he thought, were useless and improper "in a *Popular Auditory*."[13]

For a variety of reasons, then, no colonial Puritan was likely to write as the Anglicans did, or to admit to his work some of the elements that gave special character to theirs. Not only did he have to contend with the conditions of life in a newly settled community, but his very Puritanism stood in the way of his accepting the aims and methods of, say, Crashaw and Donne. He suspected the "forms of art ... identified with ... forms of belief which" he thought false;[14] he was imbued with the Protestant distrust of the sensuous in devotion and worship; he was awe-struck by the incomprehensibility and inexpressibility of God; he was limited by his too literal reverence for the Bible; and he had always to shape his work to suit the literary capacities of a popular audience. The omens were not auspicious for art of the Anglican or Catholic variety, but the Puritan nonetheless produced a great deal of writing which, at its best, rises to a special dignity, shaped by the essential seriousness of his view of human and divine existence.

In meeting his artistic problem he had not only a few special handicaps but, mercifully, some sources of aid closely related to them. Colonial conditions, for example, were less easy for the artist than the atmosphere of literary London, but there were compensations. The colonists were eager for books. As zealous Puritans they believed learning was next to godliness and hardly to be separated from it. So schools, a college, printing offices, and bookshops came to New England — all aids in their way to the writer; and whatever difficulties he faced he knew at least that if he wrote the truth in terms that his audience could understand he could count on their response.

There is an ancient heresy to the effect that the Puritan was "hostile" to art and that one form of this hostility was an indifference to all matters of literary style.

---

[10] I Corinthians 14:9.

[11] Letter to Henry Dodwell, quoted in Frederick J. Powicke, *The Reverend Richard Baxter; Under the Cross (1662–1691)* (London, 1927), p. 224.

[12] Manuscript, quoted by Powicke, p. 276.

[13] I. Mather, *Life and Death*, p. 85.

[14] Joseph Crouch, *Puritanism and Art. An Inquiry into a Popular Fallacy* (London, 1910), p. 199.

Actually, although there is in Puritan literature little formal literary criticism, and little discussion of the aesthetic aspects of writing, there are many passages which show that the Puritan thought long and hard about the problems of prose style and tried consciously to discover for himself a system of rules for giving adequate expression to his ideas and beliefs. It is interesting and touching to see how often Puritans, when explaining why and how they wrote as they did, confess their own shortcomings as artists, judged by the conventional standards of the literary elite. Even when they denounce the witty and overelaborate prose of their Catholic and Anglican contemporaries, there is sometimes a strong suggestion that they had more liking than they dared to confess, or their principles allowed them to indulge, for the literary flights which they professed to scorn. . . .

Finally, the fact that the New England Puritan had to direct what he wrote at an audience of plain men — sailors, fishermen, farmers, and small shopkeepers — although it made it impossible for him to write as he might have for a more expert literary clientele, called on him for special qualities of style. He knew that he must express his loftiest thinking in terms which would neither cheapen it nor leave it beyond the grasp of men who knew less about philosophy and abstract speculation than about the simple verities of the struggle for shelter, warmth, and food. Thence came the Puritan's love for homely realistic phrasing; for metaphors and similes not drawn from the classics or the world of books but from the common behavior of men and the common experiences of life; for a diction that was close to daily speech, and for figures that served to illustrate

and explain rather than to ornament or to please the literary sophisticate. The Puritan concentrated upon the means by which he could clothe his ideas so as to awake his readers both to feel and to understand. He worked to find words and images and figures of speech to which his readers would immediately respond. He wanted to bring the "Mysteries of God" down to the "language and dialect" of simple people.[15] Baxter said that he tried "to speak and write in the keenest manner to the common, ignorant, and ungodly People (without which keeness to them, no Sermon nor Book does much good)" and therefore liked "to speak of every Subject just *as it is,* and to call a Spade a Spade."[16]

But for the Puritan plainness in style did not imply tameness. "The common vernacular, the English Bible and the body of forms and images which had come down" in popular preaching "from the medieval pulpit supplied to the Puritan preachers an idiom by no means barbarous, unaccustomed or lacking in vitality."[17] It was an idiom in which "Similitudes" — metaphors or similes — were commonly used "to win the hearer by . . . plaine and evident demonstrations" and they were, like the Biblical "Similies," taken from "persons, things, and actions" which were "knowne, easie to be conceived, and apt."[18]

"The word is like an exact picture, it looks every man in the face that looks on it, if God speaks in it."[19] "A wise man

[15] Samuel Clarke, *The Lives of Thirty-Two English Divines* (3d ed.; London, 1677), p. 177.

[16] *Reliquiae Baxterianae,* edited by Matthew Sylvester (London, 1696), lib. I, part 1, p. 137.

[17] William Haller, *The Rise of Puritanism* (New York, 1938), p. 134.

[18] Richard Bernard, *The Faithful Shepheard* (London, 1607), p. 65.

[19] Thomas Shepard, "Of Ineffectual Hearing," in *Subjection to Christ* (London, 1654), p. 167.

always sailes by the same Compass, though not alwayes by the same wind."[20] The homeliness of such sentences as these makes them the more effective. They draw on the simplest material, but they are vivid. Every reader of John Bunyan knows, of course, that the dramatic power of *The Pilgrim's Progress,* or *The Life and Death of Mr. Badman,* comes in large part from Bunyan's skill in colloquial diction and his adroitness in using familiar material to symbolize or allegorize the divine. In his own apology for his book, prefixed to *The Pilgrim's Progress* (which was reprinted in Boston 1681 and 1706), he defends "Types, Shadows, and Metaphors," pointing out that the reader of the Bible is constantly dealing with symbols, allegories, and parables.

> Truth, although in Swadling-clouts, I find
> Informs the Judgement, rectifies the Mind;
> Pleases the Understanding, makes the Will
> Submit; the Memory too it doth fill
> With what doth our Imagination please.[21]

Bunyan and his fellow-Puritans knew that for a plain audience the "Swadling-clouts" of homely diction and imagery were better than the rich robes of elaborate rhetoric, allusion, and adornment with which Anglican preachers charmed the witty and learned. Everywhere in Puritan literature, here or abroad, there are characteristic images. Thomas Hooker says, "Take but an Apple, there is never a man under heaven can tell what tast it is of, whether sweet or soure, untill he have tasted of it; he seeth the colour and the quantity of it, but knoweth not the

tast: so there is no man under heaven discerneth more of grace then he findeth in himselfe."[22]

Homeliness, of course, made for realism. The world of New England Puritan writers is one in which the sea, the forest, the field, and the village household appear vividly on every page, even those devoted to the most lofty points of doctrine. Here is another example from Hooker: "Sweep your hearts, and clense those roomes, clense every sinke, brush downe every cobweb, and make roome for Christ . . . And when thou hast swept every corner of thy house, doe not leave the dust behind the doore, for that is a sluts tricke: doe not remove sin out of the tongue, and out of thy eye, and out of thy hand, and leave it in thy heart."[23] John Cotton wrote:

> And so an Huswife that takes her linning, she Sopes it, and bedawbs it, and it may be defiles it with dung, so as it neither looks nor smels wel, and when she hath done, she rubs it, and buckes it, and wrings it, and in the end all this is but to make it cleane and white; and truly so it is here, when as Tyrants most of all insult over Gods people and scoure them and lay them in Lee, or Dung, so as the very name of them stinks, yet what is this but to purge them, and to make them white, and it is a great service they doe to the people of God in so doing."[24]

Hooker writes of "Meditation":

> Meditation is not a flourishing of a mans wit, but hath a set bout at the search of the truth, beats his brain as wee use to say, ham-

20 William Hubbard, *The Happiness of a People* (Boston, 1676), p. 29.

21 John Bunyan, *The Pilgrim's Progress* (London, 1678). "The Author's Apology for his Book."

22 Sermon, "Culpable Ignorance," in Thomas Hooker, *The Saints Dignitie and Dutie* (London, 1651), p. 209.

23 Sermon, "The Preparing of the Heart," in Thomas Hooker, *The Soules Implantation* (London, 1637), p. 50.

24 John Cotton, *Christ The Fountaine of Life* (London, 1651), pp. 71–72.

mers out a buisiness, as the Gouldsmith with his mettal, he beats it and beats it, turnes it on this side and then on that, fashions it on both that he might frame it to his mind . . . It's one thing in our diet to take a snatch and away, another thing to make a meal, and sit at it on purpose until wee have seen al set before us and we have taken our fil of al, so we must not cast an eye or glimpse at the truth by some sudden or fleighty apprehension, a snatch and away, but we must make a meal of musing. [Meditation is] the traversing of a mans thoughts, the coasting of the mind and imagination into every crevis and corner . . . Meditation lifts up the latch and goes into each room, pries into every corner of the house, and surveyes the composition and making of it, with all the blemishes in it. Look as the Searcher at the Sea-Port, or Custom-house, or Ships . . . unlocks every Chest, romages every corner, takes a light to discover the darkest passages . . . Meditation goes upon discovery, toucheth at every coast, observes every creek, maps out the dayly course of a mans conversation and disposition.[25]

The Puritan's earthy phrases and images, his restriction of his material to that supplied by the Bible or the everyday life of his audience, his seriousness of purpose, and his willingness to admit only those rhetorical devices and "similitudes" which served to drive home or to make more intelligible what he saw as the truth, were all directly related to his view of God and of man. The realism and concreteness of his work, the firmness of its structure, and its dignity of tone, all reflect the profound conviction from which it came.

He had a fundamental attitude toward life which formed and unified what he wrote. He concentrated theologically on predestination, on God's choice of the

[25] Thomas Hooker, *The Application of Redemption* (2d ed.; London, 1659), pp. 210–211, 213–214.

elect, and on the possibility of the elect's achieving some assurance of salvation. He saw this doctrine as one which accounted for much of what he found in life and as one which, properly interpreted, gave a motive for a constant striving for righteousness. Thence came a great concentration on the individual's walk with God. That was not a passive process; it was a struggle, worthy of a warrior. Life was for the Puritan an epic — an epic of ordinary men, who sought by fulfilling their part of a contract with God to achieve some assurance that God had chosen to save them. It was an epic that in its day and for Puritan men and women typified admirably the problem and the solution of living in this world, and Puritan literature, taken as a whole, is the expression of it. It had special validity for New England colonists, many of whom were actually warriors, seafarers, and pilgrims. It is easy to forget how moving some of the conventional imagery of Puritan literature must have been to men who knew, or whose fathers had known, what such words as "pilgrimage," or "wayfaring," or "the perils of the sea" really meant.

No set of formulas can cover, of course, all that the Puritans wrote, or explain the variety of their work, the multiplicity of its themes, and the complications of intellectual and theological history which it reflects. But essential in most of it are its realism, its insistence on solid content rather than superficial form, on rhetoric as the servant of truth, and on "Words of Wisdom" rather than the "Wisdom of Words." So is its habitual dramatization of spiritual truth in terms of man's struggle from darkness to light. Whatever subject is to be discussed, the Puritan writer tries to make his argument or his exhortation strike home by putting it in concrete terms that will ring true in the ears of an audience of hard-working men.

Thomas Shepard believed that no one ever achieved true holiness merely by studying books, and what he wrote was: *"Jesus Christ* is not got with a wet finger."[26] The image was vivid to his readers who, when they read, patiently wet a finger to turn over the crowded pages. Shepard knew, too, about "the peace that passeth all understanding," and wanted his readers to understand how it surpasses all joys on earth, but he understood that the phrase might carry little force for men to whom toil in this world was the everyday stuff of experience. So he wrote:

Here's infinite, eternall, present sweetnesse, goodnesse, grace, glory, and mercy to be found in this God. Why post you from mountain to hill, why spend you your money, your *thoughts, time, endeavours,* on things that satisfie not? Here is thy resting place. Thy cloathes may warm thee, but they cannot feed thee; thy meat may feed thee, but cannot heal thee; thy Physick may heal thee, but cannot maintain thee; thy money may maintain thee, but cannot comfort thee when distresses of conscience and anguish of heart come upon thee. This God is joy in sadnesse, light in darknesse, life in death, Heaven in Hell. Here is all thine eye ever saw, thine heart ever desired, thy tongue ever asked, thy mind ever conceived. Here is all light in this Sun, and all water in this Sea, out of whom as out of a Crystall Fountain, thou shalt drink down all the refined sweetnesse of all creatures in heaven and earth for ever and ever. All the world is now seeking and tyring out themselves for rest; here only it can be found.[27]

In this passage, none of the dignity of the idea is lost, but the images — sweetness, clothes, money, meat, and physic;

light, darkness, and the sun; fountains and the sea; and above all the sharp picture of a world tiring itself out in its search for rest — give life to the abstract idea because they are drawn freshly from experience and applied immediately to the individual. So far as any one paragraph can, this one illustrates the best qualities of Puritan prose. It shows the operation of a definite literary theory which, however much it might differ from those in vogue elsewhere, gave plenty of scope for an artist to write with imaginative force.

The theory was not of course invented by the Puritans. Ramus had taught them to think of rhetoric not as a system with rules of its own, separate from logic, but as one dependent upon it. Words corresponded to things; the art of style was fundamentally the arrangement of them in an order which agreed with the logical structure of the created universe and with the normal procedure of the mind in dealing systematically with ideas.[28] From the classics Puritan writers, like all well-educated men of their time, learned much about basic qualities of style even though they rejected the more complicated patterns and abstruse rhetorical doctrines of the ancients. When they read current English books they found a dazzling variety of styles. Richard Hooker's

---

[26] Thomas Shepard, *The Sincere Convert* (London, 1655), p. 113.

[27] *Sincere Convert*, pp. 14–15.

[28] *Cf.* Perry Miller, *The New England Mind. The Seventeenth Century* (New York, 1939), p. 327, and *passim,* and Miller and Johnson, *Puritans,* especially pp. 32–41 and 73–74. Even without Ramus, Puritan writing would probably have been essentially the same, since what his rules required was demanded also by the Puritans' theological tenets, the character of their audience, and other factors pointed out in this chapter. Mr. F. P. Wilson in a note in his *Elizabethan and Jacobean* (Oxford, 1945), p. 137, after praising Miller's work, comments: "But while Calvinists were glad to defend their methods by the doctrine of Ramus, their attachment to dialectics rather than rhetoric is too deep-rooted to be attributed to the influence of one man."

highly rhythmical and elaborately developed periods; the tricks of the Euphuists; the terseness of Bacon's apothegms and the lucid eloquence of his *Advancement of Learning,* with its comments on rhetoric; Robert Burton's intricate embroidery of allusions and quotations, which almost hid the plain texture of his own stylistic cloth; the so-called "metaphysical" prose and verse full of far-reaching metaphors, plays on words, sound echoes, hyperboles, and paradoxes, which were written by the great Anglican artists and even a few Puritans in the days of James I — all these literary modes were used in works which the Puritans could read. They might take as models, if they wished, anything from the extreme stylistic eccentricities of the Elizabethan and Jacobean wits to the deliberately limited diction and grave measures of the King James and Genevan Bibles. Their task was to choose what literary paths to follow, not necessarily to explore new ones.

Naturally they elected to take from the ancient and modern rhetoricians what seemed to them to consort with their philosophical and religious standards and to be best adapted for their special purposes. In so doing they achieved a stylistic synthesis, not radically original or new, since its elements were sanctioned by long usage and by reputable critical authority. It was their own, however, because their emphases, their preferences for particular literary types, and their selection among accepted rhetorical devices gave it a characteristic stamp, impressed upon it by fundamental Puritan attitudes toward letters. Their writing can be understood and criticized intelligently only when it is seen as the working out of a distinct literary theory more typical of them than of any other group. They formed and applied the theory in an attempt to answer the old riddle of how infinite and eternal verity is to be expressed in the finite terms comprehensible to mortal man. They did not always succeed but, as Shepard showed in his paragraph on the peace of God, their doctrine could be effective in the hands of the Puritan artist who wanted to drive home a "lively and affectionate" sense of the divine by shooting rhetorical arrows "not over his people's heads, but into their Hearts."[29]

[29] I. Mather, *Life and Death,* p. 85.

Ralph Barton Perry: THE MORAL ATHLETE

THE present theme illustrates the tendency of critics, victims of their own wit or eloquence, to take the easy way of ridicule or adulation. The puritan is accused by his enemies of waging a war of extermination upon every value of life other than salvation. "Puritanism," it is said, is "the haunting fear that someone, somewhere, may be happy."[1] This is a modern version of Macaulay's familiar gibe: "The Puritan hated bearbaiting,

[1] Definition of puritanism by H. L. Mencken and George Jean Nathan in "Clinical Notes," *American Mercury,* January 1925, p. 59.

not because it gave pain to the bear, but because it gave pleasure to the spectators."[2] Mr. Ernest Boyd gives us another variant:

Scandals in politics and commercial dishonesty do not often call forth his [the puritan's] fulminations, for he does not conceive of the people concerned as having a particularly good time. Pleasure is the enemy, not evil, and so the joys of mind and body are under suspicion. . . . All that remains of the traditional stern virtue of Puritanism is a jealousy of everything which offers in this world the consolations advertised as belonging exclusively to the next.[3]

Let me add an even more sweeping indictment, which, despite concessions, holds puritanism responsible for all that the critic considers objectionable in the temper of American life, and illustrates the common fault of identifying the meaning of a gospel with the desiccated and negating phase into which all gospels enter in their decline:

Puritanism, great and powerful influence for good, as it once was, necessary as it once was, has also done limitless harm and continues to do harm to-day. It damages the human soul, renders it hard and gloomy, deprives it of sunshine and happiness; — in short, it takes away from the soul its joy. The Creed, or say the temper which arises from it, wrongs us sadly even to-day. More than to any other single agency we Americans owe it to the Calvinistic philosophy that we have so little of the zest of life; that our social life is so meager. Calvinism has wrought upon us and our forefathers in the Past. It deprived them not only of their music, their ballads, songs and dances, but also of all that almost infinite mass of social activity and

opportunity of happiness which goes under the name of Play, and which is vital to the soul of man, lest that soul fall into sorrow; into a barren and sad vacancy, and curse its own being. Man does not live by bread alone; neither does the soul by morals alone. It is not enough to the godlike soul to sing gloomy hymns or to dwell perpetually in the realm of a piety without joy, and frequently without mercy and kindness.[4]

As the enemies of puritanism fail to go to the root of puritanism, and neglect its characteristic truth, so friendly critics fall into an opposite fault of too readily dismissing its defects. Thus Stuart Sherman, apropos of Hawthorne:

If Puritanism means . . . fear of ecclesiastical and social censure, slavish obedience to a rigorous moral code, a self-torturing conscience, harsh judgments of the frailties of one's fellows, morbid asceticism, insensibility and hostility to the beauties of nature and art, Hawthorne was as little of a Puritan as any man that ever lived. But if Puritanism in America means to-day what the lineal and spiritual descendants of the Puritans exemplified at their best in Emerson's New England — emancipation from ecclesiastical and social oppression, escape from the extortion of the senses and the tyranny of things, a consciousness at least partly liberated from the impositions of space and time, freedom for self-dominion, a hopeful and exultant effort to enter into right, and noble, and harmonious relations with the highest impulses of one's fellows, and a vision, a love, a pursuit of the beauty which has its basis in 'the good and true' — if Puritanism means these things, then Hawthorne was a Puritan.[5]

When puritanism is thus identified only with its virtues, or with the fuller truth that has emerged in the light of history and experience, it loses its char-

[2] *The History of England from the Accession of James II*, 3 vols., Dutton (Everyman's Library), Vol. I, p. 129.

[3] *Portraits: Real and Imaginary*, Doran (now Doubleday, Doran and Company), 1924, p. 109.

[4] Langdon Mitchell, *Understanding America*, Doran, 1927, pp. 110–11.

[5] *Americans*, Scribner, 1923, pp. 136–37.

acteristic physiognomy, and the account becomes a fatuous work of edification like a censored biography subsidized by the deceased's surviving relatives. The meaning of puritanism is not fully grasped until it is seen as justifying both its apologists and its detractors. It contains a fraction of moral truth, and through excessive emphasis on that fraction, possesses characteristic defects of omission and distortion.

The puritan was peculiarly alive to the existence and the possibility of evil. He was realistic. He refused to ignore or to sentimentalize the pain, the labor, the misery, the brutality, the perpetual exposure to war and pestilence, the sense of helplessness, and the imminence of death that were the lot of man in the seventeenth century. He was aware of these things, and he did not evade them. It is not surprising that he felt that man suffered from a hereditary curse, and that only heroic measures could save him.

He looked for the remedy not in science and statesmanship but in moral regeneration. His idea was that evil, having first been translated from physical or social into spiritual terms, could then be cured by spiritual methods. The immediate effect of this was to increase the volume of conscious evil. His medicine was homeopathic, evil being treated with evil. Men must be made to feel worse before they could feel better. Over and above the natural evils from which they already suffered they must be made to suffer a 'conviction of sin' from which they had hitherto been free. This sense of depravity was the puritan's bitter medicine. . . .

In proclaiming a supreme good exalted above all natural and worldly goods, puritanism seized upon a truth; and in

driving that truth home, puritanism did justice to that truth's practical priority over all other practical truths. In its insistence upon the corollaries of this primary truth — the priority of the supreme good over all intermediate goods, the tendency of intermediate goods through their very goodness to deflect the will from its true orientation, and the possibility of achieving a new will which should flood and regenerate the total life of the individual — puritanism contributed significantly to the history of the human spirit.

But while it is proper to use the puritan as the symbol of his characteristic truths, a just criticism will note the distortions arising from his neglect of other truths. While he was alive and reponsive to the fact of evil, and thus escaped both complacency and irresponsibility, and while he rightly stressed the higher evil of lower goods, and the cure of lower evils by higher good, he was betrayed into error through the very zeal with which he was addicted to these truths. He tended to be morbidly preoccupied with evil, where a fuller wisdom would have dictated the positive vision of goodness. He did not deny to natural and worldly pleasure, or to health, or to family affection, or to social welfare, or to beauty and the cultural arts, a place in the hierarchy of goods, nor did he exclude them from his life. But in his eagerness to subordinate them he unduly disparaged them.

The inferiority or danger of lower goods is essentially different from intrinsic evil. In what is called his 'prudishness' or 'evil imagination,' and in the harshness of his discipline, the puritan fell into the error of allowing the relative or indirect evil of lower goods to contaminate their innocence. Insisting on the subordination of inferior goods, he neglected the fact that these lower goods will not flourish unless they are given room, and allowed, within broad limits, to be autonomous and spontaneous. Thus art and science and the family affections, if they are perpetually haunted by a censorious consciousness, may for lack of air be killed altogether. The puritan neglected the fact that lower goods will often pave the way to higher; and that the most effective method of dealing with lower evils is not to aggravate them by a sense of guilt, but to meet them on their own ground with the aid of the physical and social arts. He failed to realize that the sense of guilt added to the sense of natural evil may only break a man's heart and complete his feeling of impotent despair. He failed to see that higher goods, divorced from a foundation of sanity and from the satisfactions of the natural man, may themselves be only apparent, consisting in a precarious state of subjective exaltation which will tend to lapse, if indeed it does not beget a reaction to the opposite extreme.

The puritan's harsh insistence on the pre-eminent importance of salvation was suited to the exigencies of reform, or of revolution, or of migration and settlement. It put the moral and spiritual life on a war footing. It was not so good a gospel to live by over long periods of normal relaxation. Like all policies adapted to times of emergency, it curtailed liberty and impoverished the content of life. In the long run, and on the whole, the vision of a supreme good should stimulate and enrich. While giving life direction and order, it should at the same time reach down through all the levels of life, permeate the whole, enliven all of its activities. In short, the first requirement of salvation is that it should save.

* * *

In order to perfect and prove his spiritual strength the puritan engaged in exercises and went into training, much as a youth now sets out to excel in sport. An American schoolboy whom I knew made up his mind to become a high hurdler; not an ordinary everyday high hurdler, but a supreme high hurdler. He placed on his bureau a photograph of Nurmi, the Finnish long-distance champion. He gazed at this photograph every morning until there came into his face that grim expression which betokens unconquerable and irresistible resolve. This was his prayer. He abstained from candy and tobacco, and ate and drank only what was convertible into those tissues of the body which are employed in high hurdling. This was his fasting. He arranged his vacations, his friendships, his studies, his hours of sleep, his diversions, in the manner that he believed would increase his speed and endurance. Every day he weighed himself and tested himself. Slowly but steadily he clipped fractions of seconds from his record, with a growing assurance that he was one of the elect.

Now let us consider our great puritan champion, Jonathan Edwards. In early life, just after graduating from Yale at the age of seventeen, he went into training to perfect himself in godliness. For several years he recorded in a diary the course of training which he followed. Here are a few selections:

5. *Resolved,* Never to lose one moment of time, but to improve it in the most profitable way I possibly can. . . .
22. *Resolved,* To endeavour to obtain for myself as much happiness in the other world as I possibly can, with all the power, might, vigour, and vehemence, yea violence, I am capable of, or can bring myself to exert, in any way that can be thought of. . . .

38. *Resolved,* Never to utter anything that is sportive, or matter of laughter, on a Lord's day. . . .

Monday, Dec. 24 [1722]. . . . Concluded to observe, at the end of every month, the number of breaches of resolutions, to see whether they increase or diminish, to begin from this day, and to compute from that the weekly account my monthly increase, and out of the whole, my yearly increase, beginning from new-year days. . . .

Saturday evening, Jan. 5 [1723]. . . . This week, have been unhappily low in the weekly account: — and what are the reasons of it? . . . *Resolved,* That I have been negligent in two things: — in not striving enough in duty; and in not forcing myself upon religious thoughts. . . .

Sabbath-day morning, May 12. I have lost that relish of the Scriptures and other good books, which I had five or six months ago. *Resolved,* When I find in myself the least disposition to exercise good nature, that I will then strive most to feel good-naturedly.[6]

It is clear that the young Jonathan Edwards was determined to achieve perfect self-mastery and control through the exercise of his will. He deliberately set his will difficult tasks, as one takes bodily exercise by the use of antagonistic muscles. He made a business of moral virtue, felt his spiritual pulse, took his spiritual weight, and measured his spiritual record.

Another distinguished moral athlete was Cotton Mather. He was even more methodical and businesslike than Jonathan Edwards. He felt that man's moral possibilities were almost limitless, provided one went about it in a systematic way:

Without abridging yourselves of your occasional thoughts on the question, "What good may I do to-day?" fix a time, now and then, for more deliberate thoughts upon it. Cannot you find time (say, once a-week, and

how suitably on the Lord's day) to take this question into consideration:

What is there that I may do for the service of the glorious Lord, and for the welfare of those for whom I ought to be concerned?

Having implored the direction of God, "the Father of lights," consider the matter, in the various aspects of it. Consider it, till you have *resolved* on something. Write down your resolutions. Examine what precept and what promise you can find in the word of God to countenance your resolutions. Review these memorials at proper seasons, and see how far you have proceeded in the execution of them. The advantages of these preserved and revised memorials, no rhetoric will be sufficient to commend, no arithmetic to calculate. There are some animals of which we say, "They know not their own strength"; Christians, why should you be like them?[7]

It may be objected that the puritan's emphasis on moral discipline was disproportionate to the matter in hand. The American athlete is felt by many to have overdone athletics. He violates, we say, the amateur code, in the spirit if not in the letter. By his intense effort to surpass records or defeat opponents he makes work out of what should be play. He makes it uncomfortable for those who have neither the time nor the inclination to take the game so seriously. Now many people have precisely the same feeling toward the puritan. He takes his game of morality too seriously. He 'exaggerates' morality, as some colleges are said to exaggerate football. Others who cannot compete with him, because they have only their odd hours to devote to morality, feel that the pace should be slackened. They are advocates of 'morality for all,' 'intramural' morality, morality of a more sportive and spontaneous sort.

But the force of this plea for the amateur spirit in morality is somewhat weak-

[6] *Works,* Vol. I, pp. lxii–lxiii, lxvi, lxix.

[7] Cotton Mather, *Essays to Do Good,* new ed., Dover, Eng., 1826, pp. 39–40.

ened by the fact that most of those who utter it believe in being professional *somewhere*. They may be professionals in athletics, and although they think that the puritan's perpetual examination of the state of his soul is in bad taste, they have no hesitation in keeping a similar diary of the state of their muscles. Or they may be men of affairs, and want morality tempered to the tired businessman, who, however, is tired because he is so exceedingly businesslike about his business. These critics also think it morbid to balance one's spiritual account, but feel an irresistible urge to balance their bank accounts. And so with the artist, who is perhaps the most contemptuous critic of the puritan. He objects strongly to moral discipline, but devotes himself with infinite patience to the mastery of his own technique.

So it is evident that it is not so much a question of *whether* one shall be strict, as *where* one shall be strict. One will be strict, presumably, about the more important and central things: the athlete about high hurdles, the businessman about profits, the artist about music, painting, or poetry. The difference is over the question of what is important and central, and on this question the puritan held a view which, it must be admitted, is now somewhat outmoded. He held that morality is all-important and all-central. . . .

Richard Baxter, a divine of the seventeenth century, said of one of the pioneers among puritans:

My Father never scrupled Common-Prayer or Ceremonies, nor spake against Bishops, nor ever so much as prayed but by a Book or Form, being not ever acquainted then with any that did otherwise: But only for reading Scripture when the rest were Dancing on the Lord's Day, and for praying

. . . in his House, and for reproving Drunkards and Swearers, and for talking sometimes a few words of Scripture and the Life to come, he was reviled commonly by the Name of *Puritan, Precisian* and *Hypocrite*.[8]

This "reviling" became a habit and a class prejudice for generations. Said Macaulay:

To the stern precisian, even the innocent sport of the fancy seemed a crime. To light and festive natures the solemnity of the zealous brethren furnished copious matter of ridicule. From the Reformation to the civil war, almost every writer, gifted with a fine sense of the ludicrous, had taken some opportunity of assailing the straight haired, snuffling, whining saints, who christened their children out of the Book of Nehemiah, who groaned in spirit at the sight of Jack in the Green and who thought it impious to taste plum porridge on Christmas day. At length a time came when the laughers began to look grave in their turn. The rigid, ungainly zealots, after having furnished much good sport during two generations, rose up in arms, conquered, ruled, and, grimly smiling, trod down under their feet the whole crowd of mockers.[9]

What is the real onus of the epithets with which the puritan is so bitterly assailed by his opponents? In the use of these epithets the modern age is but echoing the abuse heaped, derisively or vindictively, upon the Roundhead by the Cavalier during the Puritan Revolution and the Restoration.

No one supposes that Richard Baxter's father, or any other notable puritan, went about trying to persuade people that he was more virtuous than he secretly knew himself to be. There was no notable dis-

[8] *Mr. Richard Baxter's Narrative of the Most Memorable Passages of His Life and Times,* London, 1696, p. 3.

[9] *The History of England from the Accession of James II,* Vol. I, pp. 307–08.

crepancy between the inner and the outer life of the puritan. What he professed to others he also confessed to himself. He was not distinguished among men by a lack of candor. Indeed, as George Gissing has suggested, if 'hypocrisy' means cynicism wearing a mask of virtue, then it is quite irrelevant to puritanism.[10] It is pharisaism rather than hypocrisy of which he may more reasonably be accused. Pharisaism does not mean wearing a cloak of righteousness; it means sincerely believing that one is more righteous than one really is. This is a failing that the puritan did, indeed, have difficulty in avoiding. He believed himself to be one of the elect, and that implied a moral eminence which contemporaries or later historians have not always found him to occupy. There seems to be a discrepancy between what he was and what he claimed to be. But so it seemed to him also, and hence the perpetual reproach and haunting doubts which beset him. The puritan believed himself to be called, but since his election implied an unnatural and unusual state of godliness, he could not always feel sure of himself. He alternated between the "very Top of Felicity" and the lowest depths of moral despair. It was a life of mountains and valleys with great and precipitous difference of altitude. . . .

Cotton Mather summed up this oscillation or mixture of attitudes when he signed as follows his "Resolutions as to my Walk with God": "Penned by, *Cotton Mather;* A feeble and worthless, yett (*Lord! by thy Grace!*) desirous to approve himself, a sincere and faithful Servant of Jesus Christ."[11]

The puritan may always be convicted of failure as judged by his own standard;

and of over-belief in himself as judged by his own attainment. But who cannot? It is impossible to have standards at all without exposing oneself to precisely such accusations. There is no way of being zealous in right-doing without being 'self-righteous.' To have a standard is to set a goal beyond actuality or even possibility; and yet to seek the goal is impossible unless one has moments of belief in one's power to reach it. There is perhaps no one so self-righteous as the man who is fond of calling other people 'hypocrites.' He is excessively ready to assume that he has attained his own ideal of sincerity. When standards are applied in action there will always be some concession to circumstance, some use of means by which the purity of the action is corrupted; so that it will be possible for critics (including oneself) to point out a discrepancy between the deed and the creed. A practical Christian, like Cromwell, must adjust his ideal to the context of affairs and use what weapons are at hand. A man can do his best only by confidently seeking (and perpetually missing) an unattainable perfection.

Why, then, is the puritan's self-righteousness so odious? In the first place, because the critic frankly takes the side of Mammon, and recognizes the puritan as his enemy. His criticism is self-defense or counter-attack: "In the mouth of a drunkard he is a puritan who refuseth his cups; in the mouth of a swearer he which feareth an oath; in the mouth of a libertine he who makes any scruple of common sins.". . .[12]

Everyone will, if forced, avow his allegiance to some moral code, acknowledge its logical priority over his appetites, and

---

[10] *Cf. The Private Papers of Henry Ryecroft,* Modern Library, 1918, pp. 230–39.

[11] *Diary of Cotton Mather,* 2 vols., Massachusetts

Historical Society Collections, Seventh Series, Vols. VII–VIII, 1911–12, Vol. VII, p. 5.

[12] Quoted from an undesignated source by John Brown, *The English Puritans,* G. P. Putnam's Sons, 1910, p. 3.

confess his lapses from strict rectitude. But one dislikes to be perpetually reminded of these things. When a puritan is in the neighborhood, one feels the uncomfortable sense of an accusing presence. It is impossible to go on enjoying oneself frivolously in the midst of such gravity. The puritan is the death's-head at the feast. He cannot be lightly ignored, because his admonition is re-echoed and confirmed by one's own conscience. One knows oneself to be vulnerable. Hence one hurls epithets at the puritan, hoping to frighten him away; or, if not, then to divert his attention and put him on the defensive by calling attention to his own shortcomings.

Whatever the motives of the critic himself, the puritan's moral athleticism is abundantly open to criticism. It is marked by one-sidedness and distortion — by defects of omission so serious as to amount, in moral judgment and practice, to defects of commission. Its most glaring fault is that which has invariably manifested itself in asceticism, which is only another name for moral athleticism. The ascetic treats the will as though it were in fact a sort of muscle, which could be strengthened by a moral daily dozen. He fails to see that there is no will which is not a will to do this or that. In his effort to isolate the will he divests it of content. He creates a false dualism between his will and his concrete inclinations. He does not see that if his ruthless war upon his impulses were successful, he would have destroyed himself altogether; and that it *cannot* succeed, because he can after all do no more than range one part of himself against another. Instead of achieving peace and harmony, therefore, he aggravates the antagonisms which already divide him, and converts into unnatural monsters the appetites with which he is endowed.

Similarly, the puritan in his zeal to forge a highly tempered and sharp-edged will loses sight of the ulterior purpose which such a formidable weapon is designed to serve. Its purpose is to put the appetites in their place, but this implies that they may justly claim a place. It is as much the task of the moral will to make room for the appetites as to confine them to that room. It is true that their unruliness must be broken, but only in order that they may thrive in peace. This positive provision for concrete goods and satisfactions provides the only moral justification for their subordination, as the claim of God to the obedience of his subjects rests on his provident love.

The puritan in his insistence upon the effective control of his supreme principle harps upon it incessantly, when it should be reserved for crucial decisions. Suspicious of all intermediaries, he neglects their indispensable role. Because the love of God speaks with authority, it does not follow that it must speak all the time. With God and conscience forever looking over his shoulder, a man cannot devote himself to any interest, however innocent, with the absorption which is the condition of its satisfaction. To acknowledge God's authority it is not necessary to run to God with every little problem. It is as though a man should take the Supreme Court as his guide, philosopher, and friend. God and conscience, like the Supreme Court, take no cognizance of the greater part of life. It is their function to determine a general orientation and to define limits. Within these limits subordinate principles — the appetites, prudence, family love, communal loyalties, science, and art — must enjoy autonomy. Without that autonomy they cannot be fruitful of good, and the effect is to create a waste instead of orderly abundance. . . .

Fanaticism may assume many different forms, use different symbols, excite different emotions, formulate different ideologies, but whether it be the puritanism of the seventeenth century or the communism and Fascism of the twentieth, its characteristic danger is the same. The measures taken to give a cause ascendancy, to secure allegiance to its supremacy, beget a forgetfulness and reckless disregard of that concrete beneficence which originally commended it, or which at any rate constitutes the only ground on which it possesses a moral justification.

By a curious paradox the rigorism of the puritan evades the most serious difficulties of life. His effort takes the form of a kind of brute strength rather than of skill. The difficulties which he overcomes are forces rather than complexities — forces that can be overcome by a dead heave of the will, and with comparatively little discrimination or understanding. Puritanism *wills* hard rather than thinks hard. Similarly, the puritan's precisianism involves the minimum of intellectual difficulty. The casuistical application of rules, especially of rules that are codified and set down in an authoritative document, is perhaps the simplest form of morality, requiring only a few steps of inference. The rules may go against the grain, and their application may require an overcoming of temptation, it may be difficult to *do* what one ought to do; but to *discover* what one ought to do is comparatively easy.

It is only a small part of morality which can be subserved either by 'main strength' or by the direct application of rules. Abstinence, yes; and punctuality. But temperance, wisdom, loyalty, friendship, happiness, justice, benevolence, liberty, peace — these are goods which require something more than overcoming,

and something more than purity or scrupulousness. The supreme moral difficulties are similar to the difficulties of art, requiring judgment rather than exactness or power. Strength of will divorced from the art of its judicious application leads to brutality; and rules divorced from the purpose which justifies and interprets them lead to pedantry.

If it is fair to exhibit the puritan's defects, it is also fair to remember, here as elsewhere, those opposite defects which he condemned — to remember them is to feel some sympathy with the puritan's excessive reaction. He regarded his opponents much as the youthful athlete of today regards the libertine. The lack of moral control, whether due to infirmity of will or to violence of emotion, translates itself from age to age into different terms.

The puritan of the seventeenth century had the effect of "bracing character in a period of relaxation." He stood for "the lit lamp" and "the loins girt" against the indulgence and improvidence of his times.[13] That he should have specifically attacked drunkenness, sexual looseness and perversion, the brutality of sport, licentiousness at carnivals and feasts, dancing, card-playing, was in some degree a historical accident. These may or may not remain the most conspicuous symptoms of moral weakness. If not, then others have superseded them. There is always a loose living in some sense, a laxity, a shortsightedness, a recklessness of passion, a narrow preoccupation with the immediate satisfaction, an inordinate fondness for physical pleasures. 'Self-indulgence' is a term of reproach under any code, since it implies an indifference or resistance to that code

[13] Edward Dowden, *Puritan and Anglican,* 3d ed., London, 1912, pp. 15–16.

as such, whatever code it be. Therefore he who takes arms against puritanism must consider that by so doing he gives aid and comfort to the puritan's enemy, who is in some sense also his own.

The puritan's rigorism contains, then, an important element of moral truth, both in that which it champions and in that which it opposes. He may with perfect right be made to serve as the symbol of that which he made peculiarly his own, and for which he sacrificed residual and compensating truths. So to use the puritan does not contradict the sober judgment which discovers his faults. Symbolism is not sober judgment; it is a simplification and subordination of the concrete complexity in order to point a moral. Its one-sidedness is overcome by the use of other symbols. The moral pantheon as a whole corrects the one-sided cults of its component deities: the worship of Zeus and Ares is mitigated by the worship of Athena, Aphrodite, and Apollo.

In his insistence upon the importance of salvation, the puritan symbolizes the choice of a supreme good and its preference over all other goods. Conceived as a moral athlete, the puritan symbolizes the enthronement of such a pre-eminent good — its control of the appetites, its practical ascendancy over intermediate goods, and its scrupulous regulation of conduct. He represents that inflexible adherence to creed which will always appear as fanaticism or obstinacy to more balanced minds — as the faith of the early Christians appeared to their more cultivated pagan contemporaries. He represents the ruthless subordination of every lesser consideration to the one thing needful. The puritan was single-minded — which is, in effect, to be narrow-minded. He stripped for battle by divesting himself of worldly attach-

ments, he economized his spiritual resources by reducing his appetitive liabilities, he tempered his will in the fire of enthusiasm.

Such an ancestor may properly be worshiped in those recurrent periods of individual and social reform when there is an ominous sound as of surf on the rocks. The puritan, said Stuart Sherman,

comes aboard, like a good pilot; and while we trim our sails, he takes the wheel and lays our course for a fresh voyage. His message when he leaves us is not, "Henceforth be masterless," but, "Bear thou henceforth the sceptre of thine own control through life and the passion of life." If that message still stirs us as with the sound of a trumpet, and frees and prepares us, not for the junketing of a purposeless vagabondage, but for the ardor and discipline and renunciation of a pilgrimage, we are Puritans.[14]

The puritain sailed his ship in the open seas. Despite his cult of moral vigor, he was not a moral introvert. He did not confine himself within his moral gymnasium, but used his strength out of doors, in the world. He pursued his calling, and he participated in the public life of his time and place. In the wars and revolutions precipitated by the Protestant Reformation he assumed the role of statesman and soldier. From this school of discipline came men who were notable for doing what they soberly and conscientiously resolved to do, despite temptations and obstacles — such men as William the Silent, Admiral Coligny, John Knox, Oliver Cromwell, John Milton, and our New England ancestors. The puritans imprinted on English and American institutions a quality of manly courage, self-reliance, and sobriety. We are still drawing upon the reserves of spiritual vigor which they accumulated.

14 *The Genius of America,* Scribner, 1923, p. 75.

Thomas Jefferson Wertenbaker:

THE PURITAN OLIGARCHY

PURITANISM found its truest expression, not in England, but in New England. The Bible Commonwealth envisaged by Ames, Baynes, Bradshaw and others was never established in the mother country. It was not so much the opposition of the King and the bishops which thwarted the Puritan leaders as the fact that a large part of the people, perhaps a decided majority, were not in sympathy with the reform movement. Even in their hour of triumph, when the monarchy had been overthrown by Cromwell's Ironsides, the Puritan leaders found themselves powerless to set up the government by the elect of which they had so long dreamed. The very suggestion, when made in the famous Barebones Parliament, led to the dissolution of that body and the proclaiming of the Protectorate. As for Oliver Cromwell, stern Independent though he was, his ideals were far from squaring with those of a Cotton or a Norton.

So it is to New England we must turn if we are to study the true Puritan State with all its distinctive features — congregations whose autonomy was derived from a covenant with God, a civil government in which only Church members participated, an educational system designed to buttress the orthodox religion, a rigid code of morals, the suppression of heresy. In fact, New England may be considered a laboratory of Puritan civilization.

The founders of the Massachusetts Bible State confidently expected it to endure forever. To them it was no social and religious experiment, but the carrying out of God's commands. Yet they had been in America but five or six years and were still struggling to clear the forests, lay out their meager crops and build their houses, when alarming weaknesses appeared. A few decades later the ministers were bewailing the general decline of godliness, were searching their souls for the cause of the general "decay," were warning the people that God had a controversy with them. Before the end of the seventeenth century it was apparent to all who had eyes to see that the Puritan experiment had failed.

The reforming synod of 1679, despite their earnest debates, their fasting and their prayers, threw little light upon the causes of decline. There had been heresy in the colony, they pointed out, swearing and drinking to excess had become common, the Sabbath day had been broken, love of wealth was supplanting the love of God, parents had been lax with their children, Christian education was being neglected. But they failed to see that these things were symptoms rather than causes. Had they looked deeper they would have found behind them all human nature itself — man's natural desire to acquire the good things of this world, and his instinctive dislike of restraint, whether of his personal conduct or his freedom of thought or his conscience, or his right to have a voice in the conduct of the state.

There is no reason to doubt the sincere belief of Winthrop and Cotton and Shepard that their Bible State was shaped according to God's directions and that in consequence it was as near perfect as man could make it, a civil and religious Utopia. To those who complained that this structure was undemocratic they replied that it was intended to be so. But they would have been indignant had one stigmatized it as a tyranny. Yet in some respects a tyranny it was, a tyranny over men's minds, a restriction upon one's right to think, imposed by sermons, laws against heresy and the control of education and the press. In early Massachusetts one disagreed with the minister at one's peril.

The ministers and magistrates would have been even more indignant at the accusation that the structure of Church and State was designed with the end of bestowing upon them special privilege and power. Certainly such a charge would have been unjust. Nonetheless special privilege and power it did give them. And though the ministers spoke of themselves as "God's poor servants," they valued their influence to the full and battled fiercely to retain it. In reading the election sermons one cannot escape the impression that a Norton or an Oakes or a Torrey took deep satisfaction in the privilege of scolding Magistrates and Deputies, of instructing them as to their duties and telling them what to do and what not to do. And in his own community the minister, even though perhaps a loving shepherd to his flock, demanded obedience as well as affection.

But the power of the few over the many, whether exercised by an aristocracy or a plutocracy or a theocracy, always is vulnerable to attack. If it is based on wealth, wealth may be confiscated; if it is based on military strength, arms may overcome arms; if it is based on ascendency over men's minds, reason may overthrow it. When the Puritans left England they fled from the things which seemed to them to threaten their souls, from a hostile King, from the bishops, from Church ceremonials, from lax morals, from disobedience to God's "ordinances"; but they could not flee from human nature, they could not flee from themselves. Upon landing on the shores of Massachusetts Bay they might fall on their knees to ask God to bless their great venture, but it was they themselves who brought the germs of failure.

As we have seen, economic conditions in New England — the expansion of foreign trade, the growth of fisheries, the shift from the agricultural village to the farm — tended to undermine the Puritan State. Yet it is doubtful whether any other place on the American continent would have been more favorable. Had the Puritans planted themselves on the banks of the Potomac they would almost certainly have established the plantation economy so unfavorable to religion, and have sacrificed the autonomy they valued so highly for a binding trade with England. Had they landed on the Delaware they would have found conditions there, too, far from ideal. It was on the Delaware that Penn tried his Holy Experiment, and, it will be remembered, the Holy Experiment failed. As for New Jersey, a Puritan community based upon the ideals of Ames, Cotton and Davenport was actually established there in 1666, but before five decades had passed it lay in ruins.[1]

1 T. J. Wertenbaker, *The Founding of American Civilization, The Middle Colonies,* pp. 126–129.

Even had Winthrop and the other leaders of the Great Exodus led their followers into the very heart of the American continent to establish their Zion on the banks of the Ohio or the Mississippi, the results would not have been greatly different. Though there they might have found the complete isolation they so highly valued, though no heresies from without might have filtered in, though they might have enjoyed complete political and economic independence, though the supernatural might not have grown dim before the glaring light of rationalism, the experiment would certainly have failed. It probably would have endured longer than in New England, but its ultimate fate would have been just as certain.

The temple of American Puritanism fell because it was built, had to be built, on the sands of human nature. When the pillars of the structure — political autonomy, the close alliance of Church and State, the control of education, orthodoxy, the stern code of morals, isolation — one after another began to sag, it was not so much the pillars themselves as the sand which caused the trouble. It was from beneath that came the succession of shocks which threatened the whole structure —the Roger Williams heresy, the Anne Hutchinson heresy, the Child petition, the Halfway Covenant, the demand for a wider franchise, the liberalizing of Harvard, the defeat of the clergy and magistrates in the witchcraft prosecutions, the growing laxness in morals.

In bringing to the New World a society which was largely the product of sixteenth-century thought and defending it there against change in a changing world, the Puritans attempted the impossible. As the decades of the seventeenth century passed, men's minds expanded to keep pace with new scientific discoveries, with new ideals of human rights, with new conceptions of man's relation to God. The leaders of the old order in Massachusetts might as well have attempted to interfere with the movement of the moon around the earth as to block these changes. While they were vainly trying to crystallize the Puritan spirit of the time of Winthrop and Cotton, the tide of a new civilization swept over and past them.

But failure did not bring immediate destruction. Certain features of the Puritan State survived not only the loss of the charter, the Glorious Revolution, the advance of rationalism, the weakening of the moral code, but even the American Revolution and the creation of a Federal Union. When the nineteenth century dawned New England society was still undemocratic; the clergy and the moneyed classes were still entrenched behind a barrier of statutes, patronage, election devices and traditions. In Massachusetts no atheist, no Jew, no man of meager income could be Governor; in Connecticut no Roman Catholic could be Governor. To be eligible for the Upper House in Massachusetts one must have a freehold of £300 or personal property valued at £600; in New Hampshire, a freehold of £200. "We have lived in a State which exhibits to the world a democratic exterior," one New Englander remarked, "but which actually practices all the arts of an organized aristocracy under the management of the old firm of Moses and Aaron."

It was this remnant of the Puritan oligarchy which Thomas Jefferson and his New England henchmen of the Democratic-Republican Party attacked so fiercely in the early decades of the nineteenth century. In Connecticut Abraham Bishop denounced the old charter of Charles II, upon which the government based its authority. "Let us sweep it away for a Constitution based on the will of the people," he said. The reformers denounced the clergy as a pack of privileged reactionaries who strutted around with queues and cocked hats and prated about government by the wisest and best. The conservatives fought back with every available weapon. From one pulpit after another Jefferson was denounced as an atheist, a liar, an enemy of the Churches, a Jacobin. "Let us not destroy the fabric erected by our fathers," the clergy pleaded. "The issue is clearly between religion and infidelity, morality and sin, sound government and anarchy." But they pleaded in vain. Election after election went against them, and new and more liberal Constitutions replaced the old governments. The day after the final defeat of the Connecticut conservatives, Lyman Beecher found his father seated with his head drooping on his breast. "Father, what are you thinking of?" he asked. "I am thinking of the Church of God," was the answer.

Despite the failure of the Puritan experiment it is a widely accepted belief that it was largely instrumental in moulding the character not only of modern New England, but of the entire United States. Plymouth is spoken of as the birthplace of the nation; the Puritans, it is claimed, came to America as the champions of religious freedom, they founded American democracy, they gave us the public school system, they lit the torch of learning to shine in every corner of the country, they contributed an element of stern morality.

Obviously this rests more upon fiction than reality. Plymouth was not the birth-

place of the nation, for the nation was founded neither upon the ideals and institutions of the Pilgrims nor of the Puritans who followed them to New England. In fact, the use of the word "birthplace" as a metaphor to explain the origin of the country is quite misleading. When the English colonized America they established not just one beachhead on the coast, but a half dozen or more. And it was from each of these beachheads that European civilization swept westward or northwestward or southwestward to create what later became the United States. The founders of St. Mary's, Charleston, and Philadelphia were as truly founders of this nation as those of Jamestown and Plymouth.

The belief that the Puritans came to the New World in the cause of religious freedom is, of course, completely erroneous. The battle for toleration in this country was won in the face of their bitter opposition. It would have seemed to Mary Dyer, William Robinson, Marmaduke Stevenson and William Leddra, as they went to their fate on the gallows, ironical indeed that three centuries later their executioners should win applause as champions of religious freedom.

Nor did American democracy have its origin in New England. American democracy was born in England, it was defended and enlarged in Westminster Hall and upon many an English battlefield, it was brought to America by the settlers and there given a new expression, a new growth under the influence of frontier conditions. There were noble men in New England, as in other colonies, who fought the good fight for democracy, but they were rebels against the old Puritan order, not its defenders. An oligarchy of Church members has no more place in the American system than

Locke's feudal system, or a slave-holding aristocracy, or a plutocracy based on big business, or a proletarian dictatorship.

As for the Puritan code of morals and the Puritan Sabbath observance, despite the many lapses in colonial New England itself they have left an imprint on life in many parts of the United States which has not yet been entirely erased. Blue-laws are often ignored, but they remain on the statute books. Yet it is in the South that blue-laws have the greatest vitality, and the Southern inheritance is Presbyterian, Baptist and Methodist, not Congregationalist.

A better case can be made for the influence of the Massachusetts school system, which was the most efficient in the colonies, the first to receive support from public funds, the first to be capped by a college. Yet the chief indebtedness of the United States is not to the founders of the Puritan educational system but to the men who so reconstructed it as to make it fit the needs of a democratic society. It was only under the pressure of Jeffersonian ideals that New England, two centuries after its founding, accepted the vital principle that public education should not be affiliated with any religious sect and should make civic duty rather than religion its chief objective.

But it is to the everlasting credit of the founders of New England that they lit and kept alive in infant America the fires of scholarship. The great importance they attached to learning, the readiness with which they accepted the findings of noted scientists, their own scientific strivings bore rich fruit for New England and the United States. The fact that eleven New Englanders were invited to join the Royal Society of London during the colonial period testifies to the intellectual activity of the region.

No truthful historian will withhold from New England the credit due her for her part in the creation and moulding of the nation. Her sons were among the most active in winning independence, they did their full share in shaping the Constitution, they were pioneers in opening western New York, northern Pennsylvania and the Great Lakes region, they gave the country its first American literature, they made noble contributions in the fields of invention, science, art, architecture. But most of the contributions were made after the fall of the Puritan oligarchy, and the men to whom the chief credit is due were not its supporters, but, on the contrary, those who rebelled against it.

Suggestions for Additional Reading

For those who may wish to judge the Puritan by his own words, a great deal of source material is readily available. For this reason, and because the idiom is a difficult one for the modern reader, Puritan authors have not been included in the foregoing readings. Significant Puritan writings are conveniently presented in large number in Perry Miller and Thomas H. Johnson, *The Puritans* (New York, 1938), and in two anthologies, *The American Mind* (New York, 1937), edited by Harry R. Warfel, Ralph H. Gabriel, and Stanley T. Williams, and *American Issues* (New York, 1941) by Willard Thorp, Merle Curti, and Carlos Baker. The *Original Narratives of Early American History* Series (New York, 1907–1908), general editor, James Franklin Jameson, provides us with modern reprintings of John Winthrop's classic *History of New England* and Edward Johnson, *Wonder-Working Providence of Sion's Saviour in New England*. Peter Force's *Tracts and Other Papers* (Washington, 1836–1846) includes Samuel Gorton's *Simplicities Defense Against Seven-Headed Policy* (Vol. 4, No. 6) and Thomas Morton's *New English Canaan* (Vol. 2, No. 5), both attacks on the Puritan policies. The *Collections* of the Massachusetts Historical Society contain the diaries of Samuel Sewall (Series 5, vols. 5–7) and Cotton Mather (Series 7, vols. 7–8), as well as the vigorous censures of John Clarke (Series 4, vol. 2), Thomas Lechford (Series 3, vol. 3), and Roger Williams (Series 3, vol. 1).

Two historians exemplify the treatment accorded the Puritans by their immediate New England successors. Thomas Hutchinson's *The History of the Colony and Province of Massachusetts-Bay* (ed. Lawrence Shaw Mayo, Cambridge, 1936) is a straightforward, eighteenth century account, unbiased even though written by one who was not a Puritan and who was a Tory. The classic nineteenth century account is John G. Palfrey, *History of New England* (Boston, 1859), detailed, slow-moving, didactic, and highly apologetic. For other statements of viewpoints sympathetic to the Puritans among nineteenth century writers see George E. Ellis, *The Puritan Age and Rule in the Colony of the Massachusetts Bay, 1629–1685* (New York, 1888); George Bancroft, *History of the United States* (New York, last revision, 1883–1885); and the speeches of Josiah Quincy, president of Harvard, "The Close of the Second Century from the First Settlement of the City," published by Eastburn (Boston, 1830), and George William Curtis, *Orations and Addresses* (New York, 1894). A reaction to these writers is found in Brooks Adams, *The Emancipation of Massachusetts* (Boston, 1887); Charles Francis Adams, *Three Episodes of Massachusetts History* (Boston, 1892); as well as in the little work by Charles Francis Adams from which a selection has been made, and in the volumes of *The English Colonies in America* (New York, 1882–1907) by the British historian, J. A. Doyle.

Two recent, comprehensive histories of the colonial period embody the fullest, most dispassionate studies available of the New England colonies: Herbert Levi Osgood, *The American Colonies in the Seventeenth Century* (New York, 1904–1907), vols. 1 and 3, and Charles M. Andrews, *The Colonial Period of American History* (New Haven, 1934), vol. 1. Other general histories which are valuable for the subject are Edward Channing, *A History of the United States* (New York, 1905–1908), vols. 1 and 2; Carl Becker's *Beginnings of the American People* (New York, 1915); James Truslow Adams, *The Founding of New England* (Boston, 1927), strongly anti-Puritan in viewpoint; and the cooperative work edited by Albert Bushnell Hart, *Commonwealth History of Massachusetts* (New York, 1927), which gives a broad coverage to the Puritan era in volume 1.

Further reading in the books from which selections have been made will supplement the student's knowledge of the issues already raised, as well as other aspects of Puritanism. Intellectual aspects of Puritanism are treated in Herbert W. Schneider, *The Puritan Mind* (New York, 1930); Perry Miller, *The New England Mind: The Seventeenth Century* (New York, 1939); and in Samuel Eliot Morison's volumes on the history of Harvard, *The Founding of Harvard College* and *Harvard College in the Seventeenth Century* (Cambridge, 1935–1936). In Max Savelle, *Seeds of Liberty* (New York, 1948), and Merle Curti, *The Growth of American Thought* (New York, 1943), Puritanism may be viewed in context with the thought of the colonial period as a whole. Puritan theology is the subject of Henry M. Dexter, *The Congregationalism of the Last Three Hundred Years* (New York,

1880); Joseph Haroutunian, *Piety versus Moralism* (New York, 1932); and Perry Miller, *Orthodoxy in Massachusetts, 1630–1650* (Cambridge, 1933).

The economic and social life of the Puritans is analyzed in W. B. Weeden, *Economic and Social History of New England* (Boston, 1890), and their economic thinking is treated in Joseph Dorfman, *The Economic Mind in American Civilization, 1606–1865* (New York, 1946), vol. I, chapter 3, and Richard H. Tawney, *Religion and the Rise of Capitalism* (New York, 1926), chapter 2, part 3, and chapter 4, part 3.

Further evaluations of the literary contribution of the Puritans may be found in Moses Coit Tyler, *History of American Literature* (New York, 1879); "The Puritan Tradition in American Literature," by Kenneth B. Murdock in *The Reinterpretation of American Literature*, ed. Norman Foerster (New York, 1928); Kenneth B. Murdock, *Literature & Theology in Colonial New England* (Cambridge, 1949), and in the new *Literary History of the United States*, ed. Robert E. Spiller and others (New York, 1948).

Notable biographies of Puritan leaders include Samuel H. Brockunier, *The Irrepressible Democrat, Roger Williams* (New York, 1940); Barrett Wendell, *Cotton Mather, The Puritan Priest* (New York, 1891); and Ralph and Louise Boas, *Cotton Mather, Keeper of the Puritan Conscience* (New York, 1928); Kenneth B. Murdock, *Increase Mather, The Foremost American Puritan* (Cambridge, 1925); and the sketches in Samuel Eliot Morison's *Builders of the Bay Colony* (Boston, 1930).

For the Salem witchcraft episode, the contemporary accounts are conveniently assembled in *Narratives of the Witchcraft Cases*, edited by G. L. Burr in Jameson's *Original Narratives* series. Opposing arguments concerning Cotton Mather's role are presented by C. W. Upham, *Salem Witchcraft* (Boston, 1867), and *Salem Witchcraft and Cotton Mather* (New York, 1869), both unfavorable toward Mather, and by William F. Poole's defense in the *North American Review*, CVIII (1869). A general survey is provided in George L. Kittredge's *Witchcraft in Old and New England* (Cambridge, 1929).

Some articles which add to the controversy presented by this book include those by Clifford K. Shipton opposing the interpretations of James T. Adams and Vernon L. Parrington: "A Plea for Puritanism," in the *American Historical Review*, XL, No. 2 (April, 1935), 460–467; "The New England Clergy of the Glacial Age," in *Publications* of the Colonial Society of Massachusetts, XXXII (1937), 25–54, and "The New England Frontier," in the *New England Quarterly*, X (1937), 25–36. David S. Muzzey concludes that Puritanism was influential for the development of colonial institutions and culture in "The Heritage of the Puritans," in the *Report* of the American Historical Association for 1920, 237–249 (Washington, 1925). In "The Massachusetts Experiment of 1630," Arthur H. Buffinton views the Puritans as daring innovators; *Publications* of the Colonial Society of Massachusetts, XXXII, 308–320. Herbert L. Osgood makes the case for the essentially democratic tendencies of the Massachusetts colonists in "The Political Ideas of the Puritans," in the *Political Science Quarterly*, Vol. 6, 1–28, 201–231.

For those who wish to pursue further the problem of Puritan influence on our later development, an admirable introduction is furnished in the article by Frederick J. Hoffman in the *American Quarterly*, Vol. 1, No. 3 (1949), "Philistine and Puritan in the 1920's." Other starting points might be H. L. Mencken, *A Book of Prefaces* (New York, 1917), chapter 4, "Puritanism as a Literary Force," or Ernest A. Boyd, *Portraits: Real and Imaginary* (New York, 1924), chapter 9, "Puritan Modern Style."